i

Advanced thoughts about
The Silver Lining Encounters with Angels.

"In The Silver Lining, Encounters with Angels, Gretchen Walker courageously shares her life's journey with others. It is sensitive and insightful and serves as a beacon of hope for others who have their own crosses to bear".

— Scott Sullivan, MD, FACS,

Center for Restorative Breast Surgery,

New Orleans, LA.

"Gretchen is more than a survivor-- she's thriving. In the face of life-long physical and emotional challenges, she shines with joy. *The Silver Lining* is her story of how God placed strategic people and strategic angels in her life at just the right time to help her take the next step and beyond. You will be inspired by her story and filled with a new confidence that God still works in people's lives today. "

— Rev. Jim Govatos

Lead Pastor Deer Lake UMC

Tallahassee, FL

Grateful Friend of Gretchen and Chip Walker

Eyewitness to Many of the Miracles Recorded in this Book

"I don't usually read books from this genus. I typically read books on science fiction, history, and war. However, I was pleasantly surprised how this book kept my interest at all times. Gretchen is an excellent writer and funny too. Once I started reading, I could not put the book down. She managed to find a way to take the most horrific life situations and through faith, managed to pull herself out while somehow experiencing humor. I purchased this book after my cancer returned and found me on hospice care. Gretchen's deep faith and optimism were strengths that have had a priceless impact on my final days."

— George Wayne Ricks, CPA

Titusville, FL.

"The Silver Lining: Encounters with Angels, is a deeply moving work about one woman's journey through an abusive childhood, a happy marriage, a terrifying health crisis, and a dramatic Christian walk. Gretchen writes with honesty and an open heart, sharing her deepest thoughts, darkest moments, scariest fears, and most intimate details candidly and honestly. Hers is a story that is riveting, honest, and inspiring. I gasped many times at the dark episodes in her life and cheered for the victories they produced. I guarantee that readers will be inspired by her story — I know I have been."

— Cynthia Furlong Reynolds

Author/Editor/Speaker

"Gretchen's story is an inspiration for us all. I have personally witnessed some of her struggles since we met approximately ten years ago. Her strength, talent, compassion for others, hard work and faith in God are assets we all should strive for in our own lives."

— David G. Daly, D.C.,

Daly Chiropractic and Wellness Center,

Titusville, FL.

"Gretchen Walker was a CU biology graduate who has had more than her share of medical struggles. When she was here, she completed one of the best independent studies I have ever mentored. Her work resulted in awards and publications in spite of her health obstacles. I applaud this "Little engine that could." After reading her book you too will see that she's a gentle spirit with a dragon heart!!! She is a prime example of no limitations when God is your power source."

— Dr. Gordon Weddle, PhD.

Biology professor

Campbellsville University, KY

"Gretchen is a shining example of what the love of Jesus Christ, perseverance, and a positive attitude can do in spite of severe pain, serious chronic illness, and many obstacles. This work by a true overcomer is inspiring and a potential Christian blockbuster!"

— Jackie Haines

Friend, Christian sister, and neighbor

PHOEBE A Walker

The Silver Lining

Encounters with Angels

Second Edition

PHOEBE A Walker

A true survivor's story!

Published by Mai Tai's Book Shack, Titusville

coachingbyphoebe.com

myseasidecreations.com

ISBN 13: 978-0692645123

ISBN 10: 0692645128

Cover design by: Phoebe Walker

Acknowledgements

I want to thank everyone

who has ever prayed for me

or

has intersected my life in any way;

For the Lord knows better than I

Who you are! –

and I am truly a better person

because of each encounter.

An extra special thank you to my husband.

I could not do this walk without you!

Contents

This photo was taken in March 2013, by my
friend Wanda, as one of my graduation picture
for graduate school.

PHOEBE A Walker

Prologue

Silver Linings was not an easy book for me to write because I discuss some deeply personal details from my life. In fact, there are details I'm sure my own family does not know. What greatly influenced my decision to write this book is my belief that all of us have at least one chapter in our book of life that we would rather not read aloud. In my case, I have more than I can count. By allowing myself to become fully exposed, I'm confident that not only will I continue on my journey of healing, but that it will offer hope, peace, and perhaps even direction to others. That makes sharing my story fully worth my absolute exposure.

I started writing *The Silver Lining* about four years ago, while some of my trials were still hot on the flesh. Then it sat idle for about two and a half years while I completed graduate school, and another year for down-time. Here I am, at last, ready to put all the pieces together in an attempt to create the perfect picture of the ways I find the silver lining in times of trial. Simply put, I want to share my personal growth with Christ – for that is what it all comes down to. When I learned to dance with Christ through life's storms, I enabled myself to embrace freedom from the oppressing elements of each trial, one at a time. My hope is that no matter how dark your trials get, you too will be able to look up and find your own silver linings.

In the difficulty of my walks, I quickly realized that if I obsessed about the situation, then I stayed there. Ultimately, this meant Satan won and I was miserable. By recognizing each tumble, I become an inspiration to myself—and my hope is that it overflows to others as well. Yes, sometimes we need to give ourselves permission to wallow in the trials for a night (or a couple days), but then we need to get up, brush off our rear ends, and set goals to work towards. But lets face it: most of us can't get from our rear end to a standing position in a single move. It often takes multiple steps to successfully maneuver out of trials and into triumphs. This book clearly relays a pattern from my own life: I wallow, God presents me with tools or people, then I become motivated to move forward. I encourage you to not lose the forward momentum. If that happens it's time to assess what went wrong and try again.

Throughout this book you will see me make reference to medical procedures and diseases. I am not an expert in either of these areas. What I have written here is solely based on my personal experiences. Please do not take my references as expert advice.

Lastly, when reading about silver linings, keep in mind what I have learned: that silver linings will probably be different for each situation. Most of all, realize that it takes a hardship or trial to even have need for a silver lining.

I bid you well on your search for your own silver linings. May my examples prepare you to better identify them in your time of need.

Blessings to you!

-   Phoebe

Chapter 1

In the Beginning, Finding God

"Gretchen, do you know Christ?" My best friend, Cristi asked, sitting on her bed in the semi-darkness of a sleepover after my sophomore year in high school. The question sparked a personal reflection. I'd weathered sixteen years of hardships on my own—my mother's constant verbal and physical abuse, promiscuity, bullies in elementary school—could I use an ally like God to walk with me through the next sixteen years? My answer was, most definitely yes.

That was early June 1989 when Cristi verbally guided me through my first spiritual life change. It was a decision that held deep eternal reward and changed the course of my life forever. First, let me rewind to tell a little about how I grew to this moment.

My earliest memories date back to when I was my daddy's three-year-old little princess. It is amazing to look back now and think of how much my three-year-old mind could already comprehend the lack of love from one parent—namely, my mother. I believe that realization not only created a deep confusion that lasted throughout my young life, it also caused a peculiarity in my persona. The only person who seemed to stabilize me was my dad. I can with all certainty call him my first silver lining.

My daddy called me his "little pinky" because I was tiny and wanted everything to be pink, even at times, my food. My dad had a short stalky body shape, but I looked up at him as if he had a tall and strong stature suited for a king. He didn't have great physical strength, but he certainly had a strongly tenacious voice. However, when he handled me in my younger years, he did so with a nurturing, gentle, and loving touch. I believed those traits were necessary for him to properly protect his little princess. Me.

My dad was the pastor of an older Presbyterian church that was located directly across the street from our house. I thought that old church looked just like a gigantic castle, which made it easy for me to fantasize this way. I made my daddy the ruler over the castle and the kingdom that surrounded it. Of course, in my little mind, the entire kingdom only stretched to the block that surrounded the church and the block that surrounded our house.

My grandma on my dad's side knew I was the child who needed a bit more attention. While I did not intentionally seek it, my subconscious must have made it evident to her because every time I saw her, she intentionally made private time for the two of us. This occurred about once a year and sometimes twice, each year until she passed away. I imagine this is what contributed to my above-average excitement about visiting with her.

Our alone time generally started with me sitting in her lap while she rocked with me in the rocking chair and gently patted my bum.

This is when she told me a story, always the same one. It went something like this. Years ago, there was a handsome young man who found his beautiful maiden. They fell in love and got married. She was referring to my parents here. Several years later, the fair maiden gave birth to a beautiful baby girl that they cherished together. That was my older sister.

Three years later, that same maiden went to the hospital to deliver their second child. She delivered a baby boy. What joy! She had the perfect family, with one boy and one girl. A few minutes later, to the couple's surprise, the maiden went into labor again and delivered another child. A beautiful baby girl. The maiden did not know she had been pregnant with twins until that moment.

You would have thought the maiden would be overjoyed with another baby, but that little girl did not get the same reception as her twin brother. In fact, the maiden focused most of her attention on the older sister and the twin brother. I know you must be feeling badly for that sweet little bundle of joy but you should not, for she had a daddy who went to her side whenever he felt she needed him. That man loved all three of his children very dearly, but he also knew this one was delicate and needed him in a different way than her other siblings did. For this reason, he spent a little extra time with this one.

After my grandmother finished the story, she would give me a big squeeze, kiss me on the head, and say, "This is the story of your family. *You* are the youngest baby girl." Of course, she adapted the story many years later, after my two half-brothers came along when I officially became the middle child.

My grandmother was very open about telling me that I was born for my dad. She reminded me of this fact until she died the year I turned thirty. In fact, she was not the only one who alluded to that over the years. I have had family members on both sides of my family who told me that they remember my dad taking care of me the majority of the time.

When I think back to the early memories of my daddy being the king, my mother was always the bad person. In fact, many times I looked at her as the wicked stepmother or witch who only wished to do me harm. While I desperately wanted a "mommy," I was afraid of my mom and almost daily went to my dad to tell on her, describing how she was so mean to me. I used to dream that somehow, she would go away and a nice sweet mommy would replace her. Imagine what went through my head when my parents got divorced four years later, the summer I turned seven.

I blamed myself for wishing they would split up. I felt I was responsible for breaking up the family. I wondered how anyone could love me after I caused so much brokenness. Fortunately, I could talk to my paternal grandmother. She was like my fairy godmother and always knew the right things to say to make me feel better. Grandma was my second silver lining.

After I heard about the divorce, I called her to talk about it. She said, "Listen to what I am about to tell you, and never forget. This situation is not your fault. You are more special than you can ever know." She went on to remind me that God must have put me here to be my dad's baby. My grandma told me that my mom was so focused on my brother and sister that my dad was my primary care giver, at least every time Grandma saw us. He had enough love for me to cover both parents, she said.

That made sense to me. I remembered strangers commenting that I must not have had any legs of my own because my daddy was always carrying me. Then, when I finally let him put me down, I clung to his legs so I could easily hide behind them.

After my parents were divorced in 1980, my siblings and I moved into a two-story apartment in Indianapolis with our mom. Have you ever been in a situation so dreadful that you wanted to hold your breath until you got through it? Well, that was how I felt for the five years that we lived in that apartment. Both my brother and sister had friends and spent as much time away from home as they could. I spent the majority of time at the apartment because I did not have any friends nearby.

After the divorce, my mother became a very angry person, and she vented her anger by yelling all the time with physical brutality. My sister was the oldest sibling, so my mother leveraged many responsibilities on her including dinner preparations and care for my brother and me. It seemed anytime something went wrong with those added responsibilities my mother went after her. She used my sister's long hair as a tool to smash her against the wall. Then my mother pinned her against the wall while she punched and kicked my sister.

The pretty hedges around the back porch had a sinister meaning for my brother and me. My mother was always finding a reason to order us to cut our own switches from those plants so she could whip us.

One day my brother and I became so upset about the whippings without reason that we dug up every one of those plants—at least a dozen of them. We not only dug them up, but we cut all the branches off the main sections, carried them out the gate and down about 200 feet to the end of the six-foot fence behind our apartment. We stacked the branches behind that fence in a wooded area. When our mother returned home, she cried and screamed. "Those were my favorite plants, they were beautiful and so expensive," she bellowed. They obviously meant more to her than her children did. You would have thought we crushed her world, she was that angry. I thought she would never stop screaming at us that night.

Unfortunately, removing those hedges did not stop the corporal punishment. She continued using her fists, feet, and kitchen utensils when she was upset. I believe this abuse, coupled with the bullying from kids at school, led to my academic struggles. Many years I barely passed into the next grade.

While we lived at this apartment, I had a very close relationship with my twin brother. I hoped it would always stay that way. Unfortunately, it did not. Now that we are older, I pray often that one day we can rebuild our close relationship because I know he was a major silver lining for me when we were young.

I oftentimes cried as I watched my twin brother wrongly punished for something he didn't do. The worst incident was when he decided to take the blame for something I did. I can't remember what I did that made my mother angry this time. However, just days before, she had dragged me up the stairs by my ear while kicking and hitting me. "She's going to pull my ear off my head before we reach the top step," I thought to myself. My brother knew days later that I still had a great deal of pain and he wanted to protect me from another round of punishment. I was grateful he wanted to do that for me but I worried about what she would do to him.

My bedroom door was situated all the way to the right on the wall. Directly to the left of the door was the closet that my sister and I shared. It had three sliding mirrored doors that stretched the remaining length of that wall.

I remember watching with fear while wishing I could make us both disappear, when my mom started punishing my brother for something I had done. I was sitting on the floor next to the door, with my feet wrapped along the wall into the closet. I guess you could say I felt some level of safety in that confined space.

As I watched the abuse through my cracked-open bedroom door, I thought my mother was going to kill my brother. He was writhing in the fetal position on the floor next to the stairs, but she kept kicking and punching him. I could not control my own crying. I wanted to run out and start hitting her to make her stop. Finally, after a while, she clumped downstairs. I snuck down the hallway to my brother's room to see if he was okay. I found him on his bed inspecting all of his wounds. I told him thank you for taking that lashing and explained my regret for what he endured for me. When I returned to my room, I climbed into a corner of my closet, where I hid for protection and cried.

I spent many hours at least once a week in that space— whenever my mother vented her anger. The closet was dark and quiet. It made me feel like I was under a cloak of invisibility.

I did not really have friends near this apartment. The one girl I considered a good friend lived about three miles down the road, too far for me to walk. I know this because I tried it once and gave up halfway there.

Most of the other kids at school were brutally mean to me. They made fun of me for the clothes my mom made me wear, which greatly resembled something you would see on "Little House on the Prairie." Everything I had was outdated—embarrassingly so. Many times I hoped my brother would protect me. Several times he told those bullies, "Don't say that to her, she's my sister. I am the only one that's allowed to say those things about her."

The kids at school who always picked on me persisted in threatening to meet me after school and beat me up. I was by far, the smallest of them being under four feet tall and less than fifty pounds. I did not know the first thing about fighting, but I knew that a war was being waged against me, both at school and at home.

I finally got tired of it and worked up my courage to meet those girls behind my apartment complex. When the tall skinny girl shoved me, I pushed back. Hard enough for her to fall on the ground and lose her glasses. When she got up, she ran home with her friends following right behind. They didn't bother me again after that. However, my victories were few and far between during these five years, so I took what I could get.

My mother hated my father so much that she manufactured games to torment him, using my siblings and me as pawns. For example, one time, my father's second wife came to pick us up for the weekend. When she parked in front of our apartment, instead of coming to the door to get us, she honked her car horn. I remember feeling relief when I heard the horn because I desperately wanted to leave. Then, my mom told us we were not done with our chores, so we could not leave the house until we completed the work. That only made me work faster.

Our stepmom waited over thirty minutes and then drove a half-hour drive back home to get my father. She did not know why we were not coming to the car. When my father arrived at our apartment, he was very upset. We missed the meal that night at Dad's house, thanks to our mother's behavior. We were sent to bed after a dinner of toast, water, and vitamins. I remember feeling so angry with my mother and asking myself, "Why didn't Dad understand that it was Mom's fault, not ours?" I didn't understand the dynamics then, but the reality is that this type of event occurred not because of anything my siblings and I had done, but because of the animosity my parents had for each other.

I cannot begin to describe how much I hated life between the second and sixth grades. At least once a year I attempted to move in with my dad, but my mom would never let that happen. When that failed, I tried running away, but I didn't know where to run. Many times, I thought about living in that wooded area behind our apartment complex, but the devil worshiper shrines set up out there terrified me. I decided I would just have to bide my time until the day I could move in with my dad.

<hr />

After living in the apartment complex for five years, my mom got married and we moved to Lebanon, Indiana. That was in 1985, just as I was starting seventh grade. The house we moved into belonged to my mom's new husband. I was relieved to have a new start, with so many other kids who were new to the same school. My brother and I naturally migrated in with the new-student group. Unfortunately, my brother and I became so active with friends that we didn't talk so much.

I tried to develop a relationship with my sister, thinking it would be easy because were older and still shared a room. I remember watching her and daydreaming about what it would be like to be her. She had a car. She was an honors student at the high school. And she worked when she was not participating in school activities. The car and the job gave my sister independence, which I believed made her life better than mine. I hoped that if I followed in her steps, I might be able to escape the hell I was living.

Many years later, when we were adults, my sister shared with me how difficult her life was too; memories I had suppressed. However, she was in a better position to get out because she was older and could work. My sister told me that she worked very hard to save money so she could get out of our *house of horrors* as soon as possible. That explained why I did not see her often. Today, we do not talk as often as I would like, but at least we are working on connecting more.

Fortunately, it did not take me long to develop genuine relationships with a small group of friends. Kids at Lebanon Middle School were not nearly as mean as those in the Indianapolis school. Although the popular kids still treated me as a dorkie nerd, my friends treated me well, so the rude gestures and comments from the popular kids didn't bother me as much. I knew my friends had an abundance of love for me, and that gave me a sense of belonging with them. This group of friends formed my next silver lining. I don't believe I would have had the strength to function if not for them.

What bothered me the most after this move was that my mom continued to be physically aggressive with me. On my thirteenth birthday, she saw me in the hallway and punched me hard in the arm because one of my friends had arrived at my birthday party early. For the first time, I punched her back. "Never punch me again," I yelled. "I'm not your personal beating bag!" That was the first time I stood up to her.

Sometimes I called my mom a brainwasher. She tried to fill my head with horrible ideas about my dad. She would order me to call him and say that I refused to go to his house for my regular bi-monthly visit. I can't remember how old I was, but the one time I did this, my dad was so angry he came into my mother's house looking for me. My mom told me to hide in my bedroom, that she would not let him in. She lied. Not only did he come in, but he started yelling at me about how I had hurt him for refusing to visit on a weekend when his family was there. I did go with him and tried desperately to stay after I got there, but I had to return to my mom's house. Begrudgingly.

During the years when I lived with my mom, I never felt safe and I always felt powerless to get out of my situation. My response was to isolate myself, lying to avoid punishment, and creating imaginary realities that were safe. After a while, I started hearing my siblings talk about my peculiar behavior.

One of my friends lived with her mom right around the corner from me. Both of our mothers smoked cigarettes, and the two of us would steal a pack and head to a small bridge where trains crossed a creek in the back of our neighborhood. We would sit under that bridge and talk for hours about our lives and struggles. One day she invited me to church, something my mother never did. The only time I went to church was during the twice-a-month visits to my dad's house.

I cannot remember the type of church it was, but I do remember that I could get there without asking anyone for a ride, because the church van picked us up. God reached me there and let me know I was important. I only attended the church a few times, but the impact was profound. It was the first time I started talking to other adults about the activities in my house that made me feel threatened. Church leaders felt convicted to lay hands on me and pray. I received a divine level of peace and emotional strength through their blessings—and I needed that help, to deal with my mother's abuse.

Not only did my mother abuse me psychologically and physically, but my stepdad began touching me inappropriately. The first time was shortly after my mom asked him to stay overnight with her. I was eight years old and in third grade.

The man would kneel on the floor and start tickling me. The first time I thought maybe he meant to grab my inner thigh and missed, but his probing touch happened every time he played that game. I told him I didn't like what he was doing. But he continued.

During the winters, on very cold nights, the skin on my back would get dry enough to crack. My mom would ask the man to put lotion on my back. He had me lie face-down on my mother's bed, then he would push my shirt all the way up over my shoulders. While he applied the lotion, I always felt his hands creep between my arms and my side then down to the front. I started squeezing my arms tight against my sides to stop him from doing that, in case it was an accident. In this way, I told myself, I would let him know he was not in the right place. But my efforts didn't stop him. He just pushed harder to move his hands where he wanted them to go.

During the summer 1988, after I completed my freshman year of high school, I was in the attic when my stepdad was working up there. I positioned myself to start my ascent down the ladder when he grabbed me in a completely inappropriate location. "Don't touch me there again," I shouted at him.

"What? I was just trying to keep you from falling," he said.

I snapped back, "I was not even on the ladder yet."

As soon as I could, I rushed to the phone and pleaded with my dad to come get me right away. "Please," I begged. "I can't live here anymore. I need you to get me." I told him I'd be waiting at the end of the driveway.

"I'm on the way," Dad said.

I packed a few clothes, stuffed animals, and special trinkets from friends, enough to fill two medium sized cardboard boxes, and carried them to the end of my driveway. On the way out the door the last time, I turned to my mother and told her, "If you'd have put out more for your husband, he wouldn't think he had to get it from me." I did not listen for a response as I walked to the driveway where I sat on the boxes and waited for my father to arrive.

While I waited for my dad to make his thirty minute drive, my mom came outside crying and begging me to come back into the house. She told me that she would call my dad and tell him not to come and she would help me unpack. Without looking at her, I sharply stated, "My things are packed. These boxes are not coming unpacked until they're in a new home." She gave up before my dad arrived, and went inside. I did not see her again for years. This same summer, my sister moved into her own apartment and my brother stopped his regular visitation with our dad. The only part I regret was that I left without saying good-bye to my friends or my siblings. I walked out and did not turn back. Fortunately, in recent years, several of those middle school friends have found me on Facebook.

Because I left without saying goodbye or telling my brother and sister what happened, my mother could lie to them about why I left and what happened. For years I didn't know what she said, but I knew it wasn't good. My brother stopped talking to me. Finally, to my great relief, we spoke on the phone before my first marriage, and he told me what our mother had said to him. All terrible lies. Unfortunately, since I didn't know how to prove my innocence to my brother, our relationship remained strained for several more years.

The first night at my dad's house, I explained to my father what happened that caused me to call for help. I told him that no adult intervened with the abuse--no neighbors, clergy, or teachers. After the talk, I don't even think my dad took any actions against my mother or stepfather. However, he told me that he called my mom and threatened action if it ever happened again. My dad also promised that I would never again have to return to my mom's house. However, that promise, did not stop her from calling his house to speak with me. Or, more accurately, to torment me. She called to inform me, in words not worthy of repeating, that I was sleeping around and would not amount to anything. Many times, I just hung up on her and immediately informed my dad, so he could deal with it. However, I am not sure he ever did.

During all those years while I lived with my mother, so many people said horrible things to and about me that I started to believe what they were saying. I withdrew from everyone, almost to the point of becoming a recluse. Whenever things were not going well, I felt as if someone pushed a button on my back; instantly those horrible statements replayed in my head. I started believing the lies and drew myself as inward as I could in my attempt to become invisible. I felt filthy, not worthy of being near anyone, and completely deserving of what harm came to me. My futile attempts to escape those lies found me creating false realities for comfort. I lived in a made-up fantasy world. Not only was it tiring, but this created identity made me feel as if I was not a real person. That way of living lasted through most of my young life.

Fortunately, when I moved in with my dad, I realized I desperately needed to stop believing those lies. Much like Sleeping Beauty, it was time to wake up and start living life. Even before I realized it, I knew God was protecting me. Definitely, when I look back now, I see it. However, during those young years, I didn't know how to start living the right life. Yet I believed God endowed me with a tool to make it through these struggles. It was my survivor's heart that was receptive to Him even before I called Him God. This strong mentality to fight for survival is how I walked with baby steps out of the oppression at my mom's house.

One of the first great joys of moving into my dad's house was female step-cousins in my age group. Julie and Jenny McClung were like instant friends, though Julie was the one I spent the most time with. I shared my stories with her. I can honestly say that she was one of my early silver linings during a time when I was processing the shift from my mom's to my dad's house. However, I enjoyed talking to both of them because we were in the same situation: girls whose fathers married into the same fantastic family. We did not get to spend much time together, but when we did, it was fun to compare our notes of being stepdaughters. I remember the three of us felt largely blessed through interactions within our stepmothers' family.

My dad had preached in Presbyterian churches. After he married Sherry, she introduced us to the Moravian church. My first major influence after moving in with my dad in 1988 was the weeklong Moravian youth camp where Dad sent me. This took place during spring break April 1989. Julie went too. I did not feel alone because I knew someone there. For the first time, I was in a safe place, where I could openly talk about anything and not get hurt. However, I only opened up a little.

I believe this opportunity helped me put my life into perspective. Most importantly, it allowed me to see how much God loved me. I cannot remember all of the activities that I participated in that summer, but I do remember how many times we talked about God and knowing the truth. This helped me start discerning truth from the lies people had told me. The closing ceremony was powerful. One of the pastors portrayed Jesus hanging on a cross for our sins—even sins against us. I realized that if Jesus was willing to die on a cross for everyone's sins, then I should be able to forgive those who had sinned against me.

I could feel healing starting to take place within me.

During the fall of 1988, I started sophomore year in high school at a performing theater arts school, Broad Ripple High, in Broad Ripple Indiana. No one there knew me; I could become anyone I wanted to become. During the summer before this term, my dad paid for modeling classes, which significantly increased my self-confidence and reduced my shyness. The first day of school, I decided I needed to smile at everyone and start with "Hello." That day I was amazed to learn how successful a smile and hello could be for me. I made several friends before I went home.

During this year, I joined the track and field team, and discovered a great interest in drawing and acting. There are no words to describe the feeling I had while being able to explore my likes and abilities. In addition to identifying recreational interests, I realized that I loved school. My academics started to soar. I even participated in advanced placement classes. These things helped me realize how oppressed I had been while living with my mom.

Sophomore year got even better. I met Cristi Clock. She was in the eleventh grade, skinny, and much taller than I was. She had the most beautiful long, extra-curly blond hair and looked a great deal like Alice in Wonderland. We met in Mrs. Merchant's geometry class. This teacher had a reputation for being very mean. Students did not want to be in her class. We all felt like she was out to flunk us, though I think I actually started to like her by the end of the term. I remember Cristi and I struggled together through this class and thankfully came out passing on the other side. The best part of the course was that I met Cristi.

<hr />

It was wonderful to move in with my dad. However, there was so much demand on his time from outside of the house. He owned his own marriage and family counseling practice. When I saw him, it was usually late at night, after he returned home and I completed my homework. My favorite nights were those when he prepared a pot of

Campbell's tomato soup and grilled cheese sandwiches cut into finger-like slices. He made enough for the two of us to share and we took that time to catch up. I still get misty-eyed when I think about those very special connections.

Unfortunately, they did not happen often enough. While I no longer had the oppression I had suffered under my mom's roof, I did not feel like I was getting enough attention from my dad. This is when I started looking outward. Several teachers figured out that I needed personal guiding attention. They gave me extra time outside of class to offer advice and direction. I also had the added benefit of my friend's parents, more specifically, Cristi's parents.

I was so fortunate that Cristi came from a fantastic family—which became more important to me than I think they ever realized. They were never judgmental and always full of love and guidance. However, there were times that I chose not go to them because I thought I might disappoint them. Regardless, I knew that when I absolutely needed them, they would be there. They let me come around often enough that I began referring to them as Momma and Papa Clock.

Okay, okay, now we come to the night that changed my life. Cristi's bedroom resembled a loft. The stairwell was on the left side of the room with a railing across the top. As soon as we reached the top step, we faced a window. With a right turn, we faced another window. The fourth wall equally divided the top floor and had a door leading into her older sister's room. The ceiling was attic style, sloped on two sides. Cristi's bed was in a little nook outside her sister's room.

That night, I was lying on the floor next to her bed staring at the light streaming in. It reverberated around the arched ceiling. Sparkles of light glistened on the ceiling above me. I thought it appeared magical, and I basked in the peace and comfort. I started wishing that was my home.

Then, just as I was drifting off to sleep, Cristi whispered, "Have you invited Christ into your heart?" With a sluggish voice, I replied, "I don't think so, but I don't know. How would I know?" All my life I believed that to ask Christ into my heart would involve many bells and whistles and include elaborate rituals. She laughed softly. "Talking to Jesus is no different from the two of us talking, Gretchen."

I was confused and wondered how I could *just* talk to someone I could not see? "Why don't you talk to your pillow?" she suggested. "That will give you something to look at, and Jesus won't mind."

That night, in June 1989, I spoke from my heart. "Lord Jesus, I love you very much and I am asking that you please come live in my heart forever and always. Please change my heart to be in alignment with yours."

I did not feel instantly transformed, but I did recognize change beginning to develop within me.

Cristi's family became an intricate part of my personal fabric. As the years passed, we discovered that it didn't matter how much time spread out between our conversations. Every time we did talk, it was as if we had not skipped a beat. In fact, on August 30, 2014, Papa Clock drove Cristi and her eleven-year-old daughter several hours in each direction so they could attend my dad's "celebration of life" after he passed away. There Papa Clock reminded me that he could never replace my daddy, but that if I ever needed a father to call on, he was available to me. And he did this until his passing January 28, 2016. This extension of my own family is an example of a very special and recurring silver lining in my life.

Chapter 2

A Divine Touch

About a month after asking Christ into my heart, in July 1989, Cristi invited me go babysit with her. The place we were going was about five miles from my dad's house, in a ritzy condominium complex. "Sure," I said. "Why not? Afterwards, we can go out to eat."

I quickly discovered that hunger would become a least important concern that night. After the child's mother left, I started having a dull ache in my right side. It felt like the pressure of someone tightly squeezing me simultaneously from the front and back. While it was not persistent, it was strong enough to acknowledge. In an attempt to minimize the discomfort, I redirected my attention to entertaining the little girl. We played with dolls and puzzles while watching television. Those activities proved successful at helping me to forget about the pain.

The child's mother arrived home long after restaurant operating hours. This defeated our dining plans. Regardless, Cristi and I still wanted to do something—anything but go straight home. We came up with this wild idea to decline the ride home so we could enjoy the adventure of a walk instead.

The start of the walk was fantastic. It seemed as if time was endless and we could go anywhere we wanted. We talked about everything that came to mind, mostly boys.

On our journey, we felt safe walking on the shoulder of this four-lane road lined with a wall of trees. Unfortunately, the farther we walked, the worse the lighting became. At one point, the night grew so dark that we could no longer see our feet below us. Just as the darkness descended, the pain returned to my side with an intensity that seemed to push my tolerance threshold to its outer limit. The situation was further complicated when we realized that we were much farther from my house than we originally thought. Instantly we recognized how vulnerable we were and fear swept over us. Our minds began creating potential dangers.

We thought about who might be sleeping in the woods and who might abduct us. Where were these thoughts before we started walking? The minimal lighting on the very straight road made us feel, at times, as if the road was actually growing longer or at best, we were walking in place. Fortunately, neither of these were reality.

About a mile from my house, one of our friends drove past us and then returned to pick us up. Though my pain was intense, I did not mind stuffing myself into the tiny back seat; it was a welcome relief from walking.

My bedroom was in the basement, and my dad, step-mom, and younger brother all slept on the second floor. The thought of their distance from me swirled around in my head as I lay in bed. Not wanting to move my body to reach them, I spent hours trying to fall asleep, but the pain prevented it. However, I must have fallen asleep at some point because I remember waking up in more excruciating pain. It was constant and sharp, like an ice pick repetitively darting deeply into and out of my flesh, each time stabbing a slightly different location. I felt so hot that it seemed a raging inferno had rendered me thoughtless.

In my attempt to process my options, I knew that I needed help, and I had to climb out of my bed to get it. No matter how slow or careful I was with my movements, the pain dramatically intensified. As I slid out of my bed, my head was pounding, my stomach was nauseous, and my legs were like spaghetti. I scooted across the floor to the bottom of the first stairway. When I looked up, I saw what appeared to be an ever-lengthening tunnel. I felt helpless at the prospect of climbing. However, I knew I had to "just-do-it!"

Tears began rolling down my cheeks as I attempted breathlessly to yell, "Help me." No one responded, so I began a shaky ascent up the stairs. Each step was excruciating as I braced my right mid-section with my left hand. I took a deep breath and pulled hard with my right hand on the step above me while simultaneously pushing hard with my left foot on the step below me. Every move saturated my entire core with intense pain. I began to wonder where this God was that I had just asked into my heart. Why would he let me suffer like this? Still, even though I could not see him, I sensed that he was there.

I tried again to yell for help when I reached the top step, but no one responded. After scooting through the kitchen, dining room, and family room on my butt, I approached the next set of stairs. Looking up that staircase, I did not think I had the energy to complete the last leg of this journey, but I knew I had to try. I stopped on every step and grasped as much air as I could before whimpering for help. Under my breath, I repeated, "Help me… Please, God, help me. You are supposed to be my help. Where are you? Please someone hear me."

Time seemed to stand still as I eased up the stairs.

Finally, outside my dad's bedroom door, I continued to cry for help, "My God I hurt so bad, someone please help me". There are no words to describe the relief I felt when my dad finally came to the door. He carried me down stairs, sat me up on the couch where he looked me over and gave me some pain medicine. He asked me to hold out a few more hours until the doctor's office opened, to save me the pain of waiting in an emergency room.

For the next few hours, I tried to focus on whatever I could to keep my mind off the pain. Before I knew it, we were driving to the doctor's office. In the examination room, the pains radiated down my entire right side and I was profusely sweating, even though I felt like I was in an ice bath. When they took my temperature, it was already over 104 degrees Fahrenheit. As soon as the doctor completed her exam, she instructed us to go to the emergency room, where help would be waiting for me.

By the time we reached the hospital, the pain was so intense that it felt like my head was going to blow off and my body was going to split in half.

At the hospital, while waiting on the gurney for lab results, I did little more than cry from the pain. I was petrified. My dad sat next to me and put his hand on my head. "Honey, you look very scared," he whispered. I told him I was. Looking back now, I believe he must have been praying for me when he touched my head because even with that level of pain, it was the first moment I felt a glimpse of peace.

About an hour later, the medical staff quickly prepared me for emergency surgery, saying they believed that my appendix was about to rupture. Events unraveled so quickly that I vaguely remember what took place between being moved from the emergency room and waking up in the recovery room after surgery.

Waking up, I felt a sense of relief and hope that they had resolved my issue. When they wheeled me to my regular hospital room, my first guest was already waiting for me. It was my twin brother, Jon. He was sitting on the window ledge. I noticed behind him that the sun was starting to go down. "Had an entire day already gone by?" I asked myself. However, that did not really matter. All that mattered was that I was going to get better now.

This was the first moment I actually considered the time of day and that there were people around. I felt excited to have each visitor enter my room until later in the evening when my step-mom's sister and her family came to visit me. I could not hold my eyes open, no matter how hard I tried. I apologized for being a horrible host because I really wanted to talk to them. I thought about how far they had driven to visit and did not want to disappoint them. But I just could not keep my eyes open to visit.

Shortly after the last visitors left my room, my nurse returned with the thermometer. This time while she was taking my temperature, I had to force my eyes open. Each time they opened, I saw my temperature going up 102...103...104...105...106. "I think your thermometer is broken," I told the nurse.

"No, it's not," she said firmly. I remember thinking how calm she was, when I thought I should be dead with a temperature like that. I realized my only option was to surrender myself to God. Maybe, I told myself, this was my time to go.

I rolled my head back onto the pillow, looked at the ceiling, and closed my eyes. Then I said, "Okay, God, here I am, if you're ready for me."

As soon as I shut my eyes, they immediately opened again. I saw several doctors and nurses scurrying around like ants on a mound – and I recognized every one of them. Who was the patient? Wait! It was me! I was watching them work on me! What was going on?

I could see my own face, but how was it that I could see all of my body from the above? Somehow, I was hovering near the ceiling, looking down on this scene.

The doctors and nurses were placing zip-lock bags filled with whole ice cubes in my groin, armpits, and other areas around my body. They had taken my blanket and sheet off and were working hard to cool me down—quickly, yet not too fast. After a couple minutes of watching, I felt myself falling toward the bed, where I returned to my body.

That was not the end of travel outside of my body. As soon as I dropped back into my body, I felt myself catapulted forward into a tunnel where there was no color. Everything was gray. A light brighter than the sun was at the far end of the tunnel, and I was moving toward it.

As I progressed into the tunnel, I felt a deep peace that there are no human words to equate the likeness. I did not know where I was and while I did not feel fear or pain, I know the question of my mortality crossed my mind. Probably more so for the curiosity of where I was going, how long I would be there, and what my existence was about to look like. For certain, the thing I knew was that I had no control over my current situation. As I continued the journey into the tunnel at a pace slower than a snail, white misty figures flew past me. They were whizzing by so fast that I could not determine what they were.

Then, one at a time, random individuals came into focus. They were people from my past who had died before me. No matter who they were, they all came to me with a HUGE smile and words of encouragement. What struck me as odd was that their mouths did not move when they talked, rather their mouths only displayed smiles. Yet, I heard each one speak to me.

One said, "God does not think you are a bad girl, neither should you. Stop being so hard on yourself."

The next one said, "You are doing GREAT and God is proud of you."

Another said, "You are going to live many years to a ripe old age and reach more people than you could ever imagine."

The last one confirmed the fact that I was not drawing any closer to the light at the end when it told me, "It's not your time, so you have to go back."

I never made it farther than one-third of the way down the tunnel, but I distinctly recall how amazingly comfortable I felt. So much genuine love seemed to envelop me, and I wanted more. I loved hearing from the people of my past, even though I could not really talk to them, conversation was one sided. It felt immensely comforting to know that they, and especially God, were proud of me.

I never saw the descent back into my body – I just found myself back on the hospital bed. When I opened my eyes, I was lying in my room, and a nurse was standing next to me. I thought I had only been sleeping for a couple of minutes until I noticed that it was daylight outside the window. Everything felt so different, and I could not figure out why. I searched around the room as a curious newborn baby might.

To my left, I noticed my roommate was no longer there. I asked where she was. "She's been discharged," the nurse told me. Later, I learned that the nurses had moved her to another room because of what was happening with me. A young girl would be terrified to have a roommate in dire distress, let alone to watch a death take place in a shared room.

The nurse started asking me questions to determine if I was alert: "What is your name?" she asked, followed by, "What day is it?" and "Who is the president?" After she finished her series of questions, I continued observing new things. There was a large machine at the end of the bed attached to a thick mat under me. The mat covered the entire bed. I remember thinking that they had to move me to place it there. I am a light sleeper, and a move like that would certainly have awakened me. Could that move have been the reason for the jolt I felt right before I catapulted into the tunnel?

I felt confused, overwhelmed by all the details I vaguely recalled. I began working to put the pieces of this puzzle together. I asked the nurse if anyone had come into the room while I was asleep. She said that she had not heard of anyone stopping by, but she would check. Apparently, since I was a minor, the medical staff was supposed to document all of my visitors, including parents.

"No, no one is on the log book," the nurse informed me when she returned. I believe the significance of "no visitors" was that I had recently asked God into my heart. Besides, I really did have a sense of peace knowing my Heavenly Father was with me the entire time. This may be exactly what He wanted to show me: that I am never alone.

After two weeks in the hospital, I could not wait to go home. What made it better was having an awesome friend like Cristi. Unfortunately, while I was in the hospital, she had decided to take a mini road trip with another friend to a party at Indiana University and did not tell her parents. This landed her with very steep punishment, restricting her activities to school, work, and home. Nowhere else. Regardless, she risked deeper consequences by coming to visit me.

Cristi was eager to see how I was feeling because the last time we had seen each other was the long and excruciating walk home just before my trip to the hospital. This was one time where I fully endorsed her defiant actions; besides, she brought ice cream. This visit instantly purged healing endorphins through my veins and zapped my energy into overdrive.

Even with less than an hour to visit, we managed to catch up on everything that took place in our two weeks apart. I believe God endorsed Cristi as a silver lining for this life event.

***

I was home for less than twenty-four hours before my temperature spiked above 104. Back to the hospital I went. This time I was not in the same kind of pain I felt two weeks prior, but I wondered whether my fever would ever go away.

Upon re-admittance, doctors determined that I was suffering from a serious kidney infection. They speculated this same infection is what caused my severe temperature that night after surgery. That extreme temperature became an indicator of sepsis in my body; the infection had permeated into my blood. Fortunately, during this second admittance, doctors were able to identify the correct intravenous medication to annihilate the kidney infection and prevent further sepsis.

Only days after starting the new medication, I regained levels of energy that I had nearly forgotten were possible. Patients in the hospital in the 1980's had little to do but watch television, work on puzzles, and look at magazines. Boredom took hold of me—but fear not, I got creative and found my own entertainment.

I started playing with the bed's remote controls until I found myself stuck. To add to the humor of the situation, the bed's controller dropped on the floor, out of reach. I could not contain my laughter, which is what lured the nurse to my room. When she arrived at the door, she found me squished between the headboard and footboard of my bed. They were as vertical as I could get them. This was possible in

1980's hospital beds. She attempted to chastise me, but couldn't control her own laughter. I quickly discovered that she had a plan.

A patient, who was just as bored as I was, occupied a room on the other side of the nurses' station. My nurse thought it would be good to connect us for morale purposes, and I am glad she did. Having someone my age to talk to made my time in the hospital go by much faster. One of our favorite things to do was to walk around the nurses' station and joke with them.

After receiving intravenous medication for several days, I showed significant improvement. To make things better, knowing my step-mom was a pediatrician, my doctor let me go home early. The one condition of my discharge was that I had to come back every day for a few hours to receive my intravenous medication until the end of treatment. My discharge day was bittersweet. I was allowed to go home, but my new friend had to stay.

Fortunately, we visited every day while I received my medication. To make things interesting, I pretended to smuggle his favorite snack items and magazines into his room. However, I had to be careful because he had diabetes. I hope that somehow during those days, I was a silver lining for him.

About a month later, that boy and I met at the Indianapolis State Fair for the first time since we both left the hospital. I do not remember much of what we talked about, but I do remember sharing my experience in the tunnel and the message God sent to me. He thought that was amazing.

Since the tunnel encounter after surgery, I frequently think back to the words spoken to me and wonder if I am staying on the right track. Regardless, I believe, with all my heart, in the fulfillment of the statements spoken to me in that near-death experience. In fact, throughout this book, you will see multiple trials where I reflect back on the tunnel experience. I use it as a faith thermometer and a source of motivation and hope.

Chapter 3

Early Growth with Christ

When I look back on how I became the person I see in the mirror today, I clearly recognize the driving forces behind both my positive and negative choices. I feel many of my initial negative choices stemmed from the circumstances in my early childhood. The first such circumstance was when my parents were divorced the summer I turned seven years old. What compounded the situation was my mother's response to me.

The first night we were in our new apartment in Indianapolis, during the summer of 1980, my mom sat with my brother, sister, and me and confronted us with the question: "Who do you want to live with?" I secretly hoped that at least one of my siblings would choose my dad. It would have made my choice easier to announce. Unfortunately they both chose our mother.

After much debate with our mother about wanting to live with both of my parents, I announced that if I had to make a decision right then, I wanted to live with my dad. She retorted, "You can't. You have to stay with me because the judge said so."

I remember asking myself, if she already knew that, why did she ask? I believe my answer directly influenced my mother's attitude toward me and led to further deterioration of our relationship. While I have asked her for forgiveness of anything I have done to hurt her, and I have forgiven her for the many hurts she caused me, we still have no contact unless I initiate it.

The day my dad died, August 28, 2014, was the last day I called her. Even though I was clearly distraught on the phone, she remained emotionless and even redirected the conversation to talk about her husband, my other abuser. I was on the phone less than three minutes when I hung up on her because of that response.

I believe it is in the best interest of my physical, mental and spiritual health to move on through life without forcing interactions with my mother. I understand that my mother had a challenging youth with the loss of both her parents at a young age. Regardless, I refuse to accept that as a viable reason for her to treat my siblings and me the way she has. Countless efforts to create a positive relationship with her have proven futile and caused too much emotional and physical pain for me. Now I feel it is pointless to continue pursuing a relationship with her. However, she is my mother and I came into this world through her. For that reason, I respect her and love her. That is something that will never change. Of course, if she initiates contact with me, I will not turn her away.

I made more negative choices in the early years after my parents divorced. I became very depressed and did not feel like I belonged anywhere. To resolve loneliness issues, I created false realities for myself—to the point where I could not keep my lies straight. I remember crying often and hating my life. The emotional oppression, physical abuse, and fears prevented me from functioning well. I wanted to kill myself.

One of my many attempts at suicide took place while I was in third grade. I climbed out of my second story window and stood on what I thought was a ledge; it was actually a drain for water. I tried to fall so that I would land on my head. This time, as well as several other times, I managed to twist at the last minute before hitting the ground. The worst injury I incurred was a bruised rear end.

The multiple attempts to drown myself were just a waste of time. The worst thing that happened was as I lost consciousness, my brain resumed breathing for me. When I could feel myself inhaling, the warmth from the water had already filled my nose and was starting to travel down my throat. I immediately forced myself out of the water and over the edge of the bathtub, where I coughed and choked the water out of my lungs.

Finally, after multiple failed attempts to permanently get out of my mother's house, I successfully moved out in the summer of 1988. I could begin a new life with my dad and stepmother. This was the summer following my first year in high school. I still have medical records that illustrate how unhealthy I was. At the age of fifteen, I weighed only eighty-three pounds and stood five feet one-and-one-half inches in height. I had been so depressed living with my mother that I did not want to eat, and when I did eat, I had issues with an upset stomach. I vomited often. Living in my dad's house, where I was loved and cared for, made a huge difference in my life. By the end of the first year in my new home, I had put on thirty-three pounds, making me a healthy one-hundred-sixteen pounds.

I felt free, as if I just accepted a second chance at life. I even came out of my shell enough to start modeling, acting, and running track. However, even with the positive life changes, many deep psychological scars remained from the years of oppression and abuse. I wanted to be near people and do what I could to make them happy because it felt good to be around those who wanted to be near me.

I made more bad decisions as I found myself doing whatever I needed to get people to like me. I became a people pleaser, which led to a promiscuous phase in my life. It felt good when young men showered me with compliments. I wanted to do what would make them happy, so they would offer more compliments and make me feel wanted and loved. More nights than I care to remember or mention, I snuck out of the house to have sex. I left from the basement door at or around mid-night and would walk around the block to where a male friend of mine would be waiting for me. We would drive to his house, have sex, and then I would return home before people in my house woke up.

I never enjoyed the act and always wanted it to be over as quickly as possible. Some nights after I returned home, I would cry because I felt so dirty. Do you remember my near-death experience at the hospital? A kidney infection caused all those symptoms. What I did not tell you was how I got the kidney infection. My promiscuity caused it. I did not know that I needed to go to the bathroom after sex to flush out the bacteria. One time, when I didn't, that is when the major infection developed.

Nevertheless, my promiscuity resulted in much more serious consequences than a kidney infection. Before I graduated from high school, I became pregnant twice and miscarried both. I believe these self-destructive, desperate times caused God to send Cristi into my life, so she could lead me to Him.

By the time I turned twenty, I felt as if I had stabilized my life. I had a relationship with God. I had a good job. And I had decided to return to college. I stopped my promiscuous life and found myself in a serious relationship with the first person who, I believed, genuinely cared about me for more than just sex. We spent more time just hanging out talking, watching television, and dancing than engaging in intercourse. We were engaged after several months of dating. Then, after less than a year, my newfound stability proved fragile. It quickly fell apart, and crashed in around me, initiated by our broken relationship.

About four weeks after my fiancé called off our engagement, Cristi saw how depressed I had become and decided she needed to help me reengage life with some excitement. We drove from Indianapolis to Chicago, to visit some of her friends there, and drove back that same night. What is better than the freedom of an unplanned road trip with no obligation for time? The trip was exciting and liberating—until, that is, my vulnerable state allowed old promiscuous habits to return. This led to a one-night stand before we drove back to Indianapolis.

About a week after the trip, my ex-fiancé called to tell me that the navy was sending him to boot camp earlier than he had expected, and he wanted to see me before he left. Even though we were not currently in a relationship, the engagement had only recently ended.

Of course, I wanted to see him. After dinner, he asked if he could stay with me that night before he shipped out in the morning. A few weeks later, I realized I was in a distressing situation when my monthly cycle was late. I asked Cristi to take me to the pharmacy to buy a pregnancy test.

We drove back to her house to take the test. I knew if the results were positive, I could talk to her parents. There, I did the whole process: pee on a stick and wait for results. Who would have thought that five minutes could ever pass that slowly? The tick-tock from the clock in the background seemed very slow, yet quite pronounced. I could hear each breath magnified in my head, audibly competing with my high-speed heart rate. I felt like I was holding my breath for the entire five minutes, and I wondered if the wait caused me to age multiple years.

Results were in. I was pregnant. And now I was extremely afraid. Cristi asked if she should get her mom. I said yes, because I needed a strong maternal figure to let me know everything was going to be okay and I trusted her.

When Momma Clock came in the room, she sat down next to me, and without a word, she embraced me. Then she asked, "What are you going to do?"

I told her there was only one thing I could do.

Even though this was not my first pregnancy, it was the first one I was certain would produce my first-born. I felt God was with me in this situation, like a divine appointment. I dedicated myself to doing what was necessary to protect this pregnancy. I knew I needed Christ and I could only do this through Him.

From the beginning, this pregnancy presented many challenges. Due to extreme stress from the difficult relationship with my ex-fiancé, I was again grossly underweight at the time of conception. The doctors did not think I could carry the baby to term and diagnosed my pregnancy as high-risk. When my mom found out about my pregnancy, she did not believe it, so she came with me to one of my doctor appointments to see for herself. Later, I found out that she was telling people that I needed to go to a home for unwed mothers and put my child up for adoption. I did not see that as an option for me.

I was unable to work because of the risk and in desperate need of assistance. My mom's brother and his wife allowed me to move in with them. This was a "safe" place to start getting things in order for my son.

First, I needed to find a church. I contacted the church my aunt and uncle attended and signed up for a new member's class. The pastor worked solo with me in an attempt to expedite the completion. Through the lessons, I began to feel a sense of peace and protection over the situation. I felt a deeper sense of God's presence and intervention when I learned the pastor had known me since I was a young child, during a time when he and my dad were colleagues.

The second step was to contact my ex-fiancé about the pregnancy. Contacting him was difficult because he was in boot camp. When I finally reached him, I told him there was a 50/50 chance the baby was not his. He chose not to talk to me for a while as he processed what he heard.

A couple weeks after our telephone conversation, he called and asked me to marry him. I knew I needed to do this to ensure health and safety of the baby and me. The proposal came just as I was completing my new member's class. It was perfect timing to approach the pastor about marrying us, and he did. Then we moved to my new husband's base assignment in Florida.

I was married and about to have my first child, TJ. I should have been a happy woman. However, my marriage was very rocky. My husband was an alcoholic who denied having a problem, which led him to abuse me, mostly verbally and psychologically but there was some physical. As for faith, he was an atheist and didn't like me to go to church. He attempted to control me by making me feel inferior and belittling me in public.

Hundreds of miles away from home and dealing with a high-risk pregnancy, I was fortunate to cross paths with Rana Strabley and her husband Chris. My new husband and I rented a small studio apartment in a building that resembled a small motel. It had two levels and three sides that wrapped around a small pool.

Rana was the resident manager and her husband was in the military, one of my husband's peers. Rana and I were three-hundred-sixty-four days apart in age, and both of us were pregnant with due dates only days apart. It was comforting to have her support and friendship in these dark early days of both marriage and pregnancy. I believe God sent Rana to be the silver lining for this life walk.

After a year of marriage, in 1995, my husband received orders to a new base. When I learned I would be moving away from Rana, my support line, I felt terribly alone. That was when God blessed me with a new friend, D'Arcy Greene.

D'Arcy was also a military wife, and her husband was a peer with mine. Like me, she was a woman chasing after God's own heart. Finding this woman was an answer to prayers because of my husband's atheism. I knew I needed God, and D'Arcy helped me find my conduit. She introduced me to the church on base.

Our first day at the church, something amazing happened as we sang hymns. A tingling sensation warmed a path down my back and arms, causing all the little hairs to stand on end. The feeling was loving and peaceful; I could only vaguely comprehend or articulate it. D'Arcy explained that this was the Holy Spirit. I realized it as something I wanted much more of so we attended as often as we could.

I believe God placed D'Arcy in my life to be the silver lining for this walk, when I made my return to Christ. By reconnecting with God, I recognized that I desperately needed to change my current living situation. I needed to get out from under this new oppression, and God gave me the necessary strength and courage to embark on the next stage of my life: single parenthood. I made an appointment with an attorney to begin the divorce process.

The divorce was difficult because my husband refused to sign the documents. He continually said he didn't like one word or another in the property settlement. After about a year of arguing the small details, I finally went to his house and told him to point out all the words he didn't like. I changed them there, in front of him, so he would sign the papers. The divorce was finalized several months later, in February 1997.

While I was awaiting my divorce, I did not want to be in a relationship. However, God must have felt that I needed a helpmate because he almost immediately sent Chip across my path. Our meeting deserves a story all of its own, but for the sake of this book, I will keep it short.

The house where TJ and I were living was broken into, so we went to stay with a friend of mine. One day while I was staying with her, I answered her phone and thought I was talking to her dad because the man had the same name. As it turns out, the Chip on the phone was a friend of hers. I was glad he was not her dad because I told her I thought her friend was a jerk. She remarked that it might have something to do with his desire to become an officer and fly airplanes, which consequently, he never did.

Later that same day, someone knocked at the door. When we opened the door, there Chip stood, as if he had just jumped out of the movie *Top Gun* during the volleyball scene. He was visiting with my friend and her family for the week before heading back to school.

That pretty much sealed my opinion that Chip was a jock and a jerk. I did not want anything to do with him and tried to avoid him by every means – until we paired up as a team for playing cards. By the end of the night, we were talking as if we had known each other for years. Something about our conversation was powerful because it left me feeling as if he was *the* one, my forever silver lining.

Another year down the road, Chip and I were married, and I became pregnant with our daughter, Ashley. This pregnancy also proved difficult. In fact, it looked worse than the high-risk pregnancy with my first-born, TJ. At seventeen-and-one-half weeks' gestation, I went into full-blown labor. In the emergency room, I cried and repeated, "I don't want to lose my baby…I don't want to lose my baby…" Out of nowhere, an unfamiliar African-American woman gently placed her hand on my shoulder and said, "The Lord is with you. Your baby is going to be okay. Trust that!"

Warmth washed over me at her words, and instantly I knew, without a doubt, that everything was going to be okay. Usually if a woman goes into preterm labor before twenty weeks' gestation, the doctors send her home to abort naturally. However, within minutes of my encounter with that woman, the emergency room staff went against protocol and admitted me to the labor and delivery floor.

That night, of the five doctors on the labor and delivery floor, all but one wanted to send me home and let the baby abort naturally. The one doctor who wanted to stop my labor was the chief of staff. You can guess who won that vote: the chief of staff. Later he confessed that he did not believe our baby girl would survive. However, something told him that he needed to attempt to stop my contractions.

Several months later, when I introduced him to my daughter, alive and healthy, he expressed delight and surprise that she survived. To the present day, I believe Ashley received a special blessing from the Lord in that emergency room, through the hand of that Holy woman. She was our quiet silver lining.

I feel that my pregnancies served as the kindling that reignited a fire in my spirit to develop a meaningful relationship with God. I have come to credit them for helping me to reengage the best relationship of my life, the one with Christ. Times were not easy, but I knew He was always there. I wanted nothing more than to see God proud of me. I should have reflected more often on my near-death experience, where I heard that he was already proud of me. Regardless, my life goal is to remain on the right path with God, to the best of my natural ability. There was no better time to exercise this goal than amidst the major life changes Chip and I were about to encounter, among them relocation and frightening medical issues.

Chapter 4

Early Signs of M.S.

When Ashley was fifteen months old, in December 1998, we received orders to our next command, in the Cornhusker State. At our new home in Nebraska, we made a point of attending church on a regular basis, at least once a week and sometimes twice. Chip started reading the "Left Behind" book series and soaked it in like a happy sponge in water. This was the most remarkable spiritual transformation I had ever seen in him as he grew in faith.

I believe God perfectly correlated the timing of our growth in faith with the next trial that was brewing. It appeared my health was on the chopping block this time. Chip was away on deployment when a large a snowstorm parked on top of us, winter 2000. In his absence, I was on snow-shoveling duty. That was not a big deal, because I acquired many physical jobs when he was on duty. This time, however, I felt physical constraints. My hands refused to keep a grip on the shovel, my arms did not want to bend, my legs felt heavy, and my vision became blurry.

In my late teens, I was a certified nursing assistant (CNA) while working toward obtaining my Licensed Practical Nursing (LPN) certification. During that time, I gained significant experience with neurologic issues. This medical experience made it possible for me to recognize my symptoms as neurologic. Since both my mother and her full-blood brother have multiple sclerosis[1] (MS), I started questioning whether I also had it.

I disputed having the disease, by arguing that cooler weather was supposed to be better for MS. Yet I was finding it difficult to function during the winter months. Regardless, I worried about whether I was starting to develop MS, and what would happen if I had a major medical issue and Chip was deployed far way. When he returned home, we discussed our options and came to a mutual agreement that he would resign from active duty at the conclusion of his current orders.

In the fall of 2001, I completed my basic associate of arts degree at the local community college, which correlated with the end of Chip's orders. Friends and colleagues from the college came to help us pack our moving truck, and we left for Florida.

When we arrived in Florida, our temporary lodging was a single bedroom within the two-bedroom apartment that my sister-in-law and her husband rented.

In a self-storage unit near the apartment, we stored all but a few essentials. We kept a queen-sized mattress for Chip and me, while both kids slept on the floor in sleeping bags. We brought some toys in the room for the kids and a television so they could watch children's

---

[1] Information on Multiple Sclerosis Society is in Appendix B.

shows. We used a small plastic storage shelf with drawers to hold toiletries and our clothes hung in the closet.

From the first day we arrived, Chip made it a full-time job every day to look for work. While he looked for work, I took our seven-year-old son to school and entertained our three-year-old daughter. We prayed often that the Lord would lead my husband to gainful employment and that the Lord would place a special blessing over my in-laws for letting us live in their apartment. When the military pay ceased, we collected unemployment to make ends meet.

In my family, I was the person was responsible for paying the bills. Depression loomed over me as I watched the bills pile up and I began receiving a never-ending succession of calls from bill collectors. Yet, what broke my heart the deepest was watching Chip continually turned down for employment. I endlessly prayed for his self-esteem, that he would not be broken. I felt hopeless, responsible for our situation, and fearful that the lifestyle we were living would not end.

In spite of how I felt, I knew I needed to hide it and remain strong for the family, especially with Ashley's fourth birthday right around the corner. It was already difficult trying to make it a special day without adding my emotional stress to the mix. Then things got worse.

A couple of weeks before Ashley's birthday, I felt odd things happening with my body. I could not walk in a straight line; rather, I oriented to the left. When I walked down a hallway, you could hear, step ... thump ... step ... thump ... step ... thump. I took a step, immediately followed by me running into the wall like a mechanical toy missing a foot. I also noticed that when I grabbed for things with my left hand, I overshot whatever I was reaching for. Sometimes my strength was too much for the action I was performing. For example, when I lifted a tissue to my nose, I inadvertently punched myself in the face.

While things were a bit disconcerting, I made every effort to avoid going for medical care because we did not have health insurance. That is, until the night of the horrible headache. It felt like I had a tube in my head that was so full of pressure that it would pop at any time. I wondered if I was having a stroke. Then, I stood up and my left leg refused to hold my body weight. It became urgent that I see a doctor now, even without insurance.

When we left for the hospital, Chip had to carry me to the car because I could not walk with only one functioning leg.

Going to the hospital without insurance was a tremendous hit to our already dwindling finances. With endless medical bills, no more military pay, and peanuts for unemployment assistance from the State of Florida, we were in a financial crisis. We realized the only way to get our head above water was to file for bankruptcy. This significantly reduced stress on me in a time where I desperately needed to reduce stress for healing to take place.

As I waited in the Emergency Room, I wondered what was happening to me. Was it serious enough to take my life? I wondered. Then I reflected on the message God had sent me years earlier, about living to a very old age. Maybe old was relative to the age I was when I had the near death experience? I debated silently. No matter, it could not be possible, because I was now only in my mid-twenties; there was no way to misconstrue that age for old, I told myself, trying to force a positive mindset.

While we waited for the doctor, I stayed as quiet as possible because my brain was irrationally answering questions about my current condition. I didn't want to share those thoughts for fear I would further scare myself or spread the fear to Chip. However, I could not easily conceal my fear and anxieties. They were as thick in the room as pea soup, in spite of my efforts.

Chip endlessly tried to calm me and lighten the mood by telling me jokes and funny stories. He even threatened to put me in the middle of the room so he could watch me walk in circles, chasing my own rear end. When his efforts didn't seem to work, he started playing with instruments around the room, until he came across the rubber glove dispenser. There he lingered for a few minutes, creating a rubber chicken that he sent to attack me as a rabid bird. Before long, I was giggling and laughing – quite a bit.

My mother-in-law, Ruth, worked at that hospital as a certified nurse's assistant (CNA). She knew I was there and wanted to check in to see how I was. When she walked into the room, she told me that she heard me laughing all the way down the hall. She knew how petrified I was because she felt it too. However, she said she was concerned that the doctors might not take me seriously if they heard me laughing like that. I was happy to see her and knew that she was sharing her concern, but I was glad that Chip helped me get my mind off the situation.

Shortly after Ruth arrived, the doctor came in and asked me the standard question: "What brings you in tonight?" I explained the symptoms, starting with my headache, then described how my left leg apparently grew a mind of its own and would not let me have a say in anything it did. During the exam, he asked me first to lift the non-affected right leg, which was quite uneventful, and then the left one.

When I lifted my left leg, we all became spectators of something truly remarkable. The leg demonstrated clearly that it had a mind of its own, by kicking and flailing all over. The intensity was so grandiose that the hospital gurney jerked around, almost bouncing off walls like a pinball game. The doctor ducked to avoid a blow from my foot and immediately instructed me to put my leg back down, but the leg had nothing to do with that request. The doctor had to grab my leg with both hands to push it down.

The doctor explained that the inability to control my leg was symptomatic of something neurologic, and he sent me for a Computed Tomography (CT) scan of my brain. The scan revealed an abnormality in the center of my brain. After determining that I was not suffering an immediate life-threatening situation, he discharged me with a referral to a neurologist the following day.

The next day we followed up with the neurologist on the referral. After reviewing my CT report, he brashly stated, "If the area of concern is a tumor, then it is inoperable due to the location." It was as if he was annoyed by my presence. I remember being very afraid and angry. I wondered, to myself, why that doctor could not have more compassion for what he was saying to me. After all, I had not chosen to have problems in my brain. I had not asked for a malfunctioning body.

Consumed by fear and disgust, I walked out of that office... still wearing my hospital gown. I changed into my clothes in a bathroom just before the main exit of the office complex. After we left the building, I begged Chip to take me straight to a church, where I sat at the altar, praying and crying my heart out to God. I did not want to leave. I just wanted to sit in God's lap, and I wanted him to make me all better. I wanted a miracle. I wanted to know what was causing these symptoms and maybe He would tell me there at the church. The answer never came, but I did find peace.

Maybe it was because it was the first place I found solace after all the medical hoopla. Maybe it was just a convenient location. Either way, we returned to that same church for Sunday service. Unfortunately, during that morning service, our experience was a total contrast from the prior visit. It was the most uncomfortable I have ever felt in a church.

I walked to the altar rail to receive communion and felt a divine peace, as if Christ was receiving me with open arms. The feeling was so powerful that the floodgates to my heart opened wide, and I sobbed with an intensity that shook my soul. It had to be God's presence in that place that caused me to sob so intensely.

Shockingly, no one spoke to or asked me why I was crying so profusely, not even the pastor. Instead, they stared with questioning eyes. It felt as if they were inquiring about what I had done. What could be so bad that I needed communion to release my guilt and cause my tears? They seemed to be asking silently. But, I told myself, their thoughts did not matter. I knew I needed to be there because I could not move without God's strength. It was so unfair that this medical situation was happening to me. If only He would tell me how to make it go away.

In the days that followed, I still had symptoms, but they became tolerable. I got used to walking in circles and not being able to button my own clothes or put toothpaste on my toothbrush. During this stage of the trial, vivid flashbacks flooded my mind. I focused on the connections I had made in my tunnel experience and God's promise about living a long time. This silver lining was God himself.

I needed to find a purpose for living and a way to accomplish it, because if I was going to be around for a very long time, I certainly did not want to live this way. Initial focus was on regaining my physical abilities. To do this, we purchased a recumbent bike that I used multiple times a day to rebuild strength in my legs. For upper body actions that I had issues with, I worked to retrain those muscles by slowing down and focusing on properly completing each action.

About three weeks after my Emergency Room visit, in September of 2001, my phone was bombarded with calls from people asking if the military had called Chip back to active duty—six weeks after he had resigned from active duty. To amazement of the people on the other end of the phone, I didn't understand the purpose of their calls. Every one of them hysterically shouted that one of the Twin Towers had been hit in a terrorist attack and was falling down. "It's all over the news! How can you not know?" they asked.

Their sheer panic fueled my curiosity enough to find out what was happening. I rushed into another room and turned the television to CNN News minutes before the second airplane flew into the second tower. Wow! I had been dealing with major medical issues and Chip's unemployment, and now this. I cried and wanted to go to a church. I wanted to hold hands with strangers and pray. The nation seemed overwhelmed with so much confusion and feelings of hopelessness.

Days before the 9-11-2001 catastrophe, we had learned that our endless praying for work had paid off. Chip received a job offer for a government position at Kennedy Space Center, and he gratefully accepted. Fortunately, the terrorist attack did not create a delay in his civilian employment. He started working a week later. With the new job, it was just a matter of time before we could have our own home, money to pay bills, and most of all, health insurance. God was answering all of our prayers. But we still had unanswered questions and a feeling of uncertainty.

About two weeks after Chip started work, we found our new home and moved in. I still had neurological symptoms but they did not seem so bad. In fact, the remaining symptoms were not visible to others. But that is typical for this "invisible" disease, Multiple Sclerosis.

Now that we had insurance, I could go see a doctor who might be able to tell me what was wrong. The new doctor ordered a brain Magnetic Resonance Image (MRI) to see if there were any changes from the hospital's Computed Tomography (CT) scan. He received the results on a Friday and called me into his office after closing time. I told Chip, "This cannot be a good thing" because it is never good when a doctor calls you into the office after hours.

The drive to his office was long, and it gave my mind ample time to fill in the blanks. Our minds can be horrible to us at times, as we try to make sense of our reality.

When we arrived at his office, the doctor informed me that there was an area of concern identified in the middle of my brain. He added that there was not enough information to know whether it was a mass or not. I started recalling the words from the first neurologist, "If it's a tumor, it's inoperable." My surroundings seemed muted as a flood of tears fell into my lap. I thought to myself, "I'm only twenty-eight years old. I am too young to die!"

Within a couple minutes, the voices became audible in time to hear the doctor say, "I'm sorry I can't give you more information than that." He spoke to Chip when he said, "Just watch her. She may start having mood swings, depression could set in, or any number of psychological issues could surface."

"Lovely!" I thought. "As if these symptoms weren't bad enough, I have the potential to become a psychological nut case too! What else is God going to allow to happen?"

I became very angry with God and wanted to know what his plans were for me. When I got home, I felt the need to hold my breath for the entire weekend as I waited to see a new neurologist. My mind refused to focus on anything but the MRI results and the report that gave us very little information. The not-knowing part almost sucked the life right out of me.

Monday morning first thing, we were sitting in another neurologist's office. I explained to the neurologist that both my mother and her brother have multiple sclerosis. He expressed his concern that I might also have it. Then more testing commenced.

In the coming weeks, I felt like a lab rat because I was scheduled at the lab frequently, having blood drawn. I remembered asking the technicians if it would be too much of an imposition to leave at least one drop of blood in my pipes. Twice, the sheer volume of blood drawn felt as if I was a blood donor times ten. Once, the lab technicians positioned me in a chair, leaning back, feet in the air, with a beverage in one hand and a snack in the other so that I would not pass out.

Being stuck with needles and stuffed into machines multiple times a week grew old quickly. At the completion of all the testing, the doctor said that he believed I had MS, but he could not diagnose me with it because I had only one lesion, a scar on the brain. Months of testing concluded with, "Here's a box of information on Avonex, read up on it and we will simply watch you for changes. When that happens we can start you on the medication [Avonex]."

After all the invasive testing, there was still no answer to the question of why these crazy things were happening--and if they would come back. I felt physically violated and drained and no longer desired to talk to anyone. I was broken and virtually told I "could not be fixed." MS is a disease that doctors diagnose by ruling everything else out. They had effectively ruled everything else out, so why couldn't they work on fixing me now?

In what appeared to be no resolution or treatment for my ongoing symptoms, I reflected on God's words to me about living to be a ripe old age. I decided I needed to find a way to live in spite of my circumstances. Remembering that people with MS could function better and have fewer symptoms in cooler, drier climates, I talked to Chip about moving us north. Unfortunately, I remembered this detail but failed to recall what the cold did to me while we were in Nebraska. Regardless, the job search began.

Chapter 5

Persevering Through the Trials

In March of 2002, Chip started looking for work in the north. Initially he searched in the very cold New England area, but God knew that would be too cold for me. A company in Kentucky, Amazon.com, extended his first job offer, and Chip accepted. For the first time in a year, our focus shifted off my health and onto new opportunity.

Time was no longer stagnant, rather it moved with a swift current. Every moment we were packing boxes or organizing items in preparation for the move to Kentucky. We put our house on the market, packed our moving truck, and headed on to a new start for all of us in late summer 2002.

I only vaguely recall details of this move, other than the fact that we moved ourselves and stayed in temporary housing when we reached Kentucky. While we were house hunting, our relocation guide introduced us to a super-fantastic couple, Jack and Shirley, who took us under their wings. They loved on us so much, that in spite of our bankruptcy from the previous year, they financed us to buy one of their investment houses. Once we settled in, I researched universities in close proximity and found one in town. It was a southern Baptist school called Campbellsville University. I applied to the biology program and received acceptance within a few weeks.

Chip worked more than fifty hours a week during the off-peak season. During the peak seasons of Thanksgiving and Christmas, he oftentimes worked in excess of sixty to eighty hours a week. Because Chip worked so many hours, I often took the kids to school with me. One of my friends also had a school-aged child. She and I interlaced participation with school functions for our children while diligently studying for our own coursework.

In the spring of 2004, I began my senior research, in Gretchen-style, attempting to defeat the odds when choosing my topic of choice in the field of biology. My plan was to complete an in-vitro fertilization of a rare species of fish. As I met with my academic advisors, they informed me that there were entirely too many unknown variables, which could prevent this research from coming through fruition. Taking heed to what they said, I began a walk that would take six years to complete full circle. This research evoked my initial deepest conversations with Christ. You could say I was strengthening my relationship with Him.

Before going into the field to collect my fish, I prayed that my team would have success. When we collected more than enough for my research, I gave thanks to the Lord. After returning them to the lab, I waited until the fish fully matured to strip their eggs and milt solution (sperm) for in-vitro fertilization. During the wait, I continued to pray, because I knew this research would not be possible or successful without God's help. Throughout my research, I endlessly prayed and in every step and gave thanks for the progress attained. I prayed more for this study than anything else other than my husband and children.

The fish were at the right place for in-vitro fertilization just as Chip was deploying for his annual two-week commitment with the military reserves. I packed our kids and brought them with me for the first day and a half of this research. About a month later, I noticed issues with my eyes. When they were open, I saw horizontal bands that rotated upward like an old television in need of a rabbit-ear adjustment. Worried that I would not be able to document developmental changes, I called my research advisor/mentor, Dr. Gordon Weddle, to check on the research specimen.

The first year's research results were limited, due to a copepod [parasite] infestation that killed my specimen. However, I obtained enough data to write my research paper. Dr. Weddle felt strongly enough about my research that he suggested I present the results at an annual undergraduate competition at Kentucky Academy of Science. He personally went to the competition with a handful of students, including me. There I earned second place for my research. "You did a good job and should be proud of yourself," Dr. Weddle said. I felt a sense of pride to hear my mentor, Dr. Weddle, complement my work. Along with the compliments from several individuals came the suggestion to get my research published. That was a challenge I was ready to accept.

With all my successes, I fully believed that God allowed my progress and would further sustain me. However, in order to get my research published, I needed more successful and thorough results. I planned to repeat the research in my final term at the university, during the spring of 2005.

The doctor prescribed steroids to resolve the situation with my eyes and I found a neurologist who again looked into diagnosing me with MS. Testing commenced with a nerve test, more blood work, and another MRI. Everything was normal except the MRI, which now reflected more than one lesion on my brain.

I wanted a second opinion from a familiar face, my neurologist in Florida. We decided to take an extended trip to Florida over the Christmas holiday. This way I could schedule an appointment with my old neurologist and have some time at the beach. I so missed the beach and knew it would help me relax and melt away from reality.

Sitting in the doctor's office, I felt nervous but believed he would confirm the diagnosis. One glance at my MRI was all he needed. "This is MS," he said. Those words still ring in my head. He said it so matter-of-fact as if I already knew—and, in reality, I did. I just didn't want it to be so. That night I cried to God, pleading with him to take it away from me. I wanted nothing more for Christmas that year, 2004, than for God to tell me it was a mistake and that the diagnosis never happened. Instead, we returned home, where I fell into a deep depression. I functioned like a pre-programed machine. Daily, I got up, took care of my kids, attended my classes, and started MS treatment.

I chose a medication that I injected daily because it was supposed to have the fewest side effects. However, after the first few shots in January 2005, I started having injection-site reactions. The longer I took the medication, the worse my reactions became. The swollen areas were the diameter of a grapefruit, and they were raised almost one-quarter inch in height. I injected the back of my arms, stomach, hips, and thighs. My body was only five-feet-two-inches tall and about 105 pounds. Between the large bumps and bruising, I started looking like a human-sized bumpy blackberry.

The pain became so fierce on all sides of my body that I could no longer sleep. During those sleepless nights, I often went into another room to cry so I wouldn't wake Chip. Every side of my body simultaneously felt deeply penetrated as if by daggers. The pain was so horrific and continuous that it was easy to convince myself I did not have MS. I thought, "If I have MS, then my body would absorb the medication and I wouldn't be in this pain."

After six weeks of injections, I could not stand the pain anymore. I stopped taking them and went on with my life as if I did not have MS. My family practice doctor agreed with my decision. He told me, "As humans we are responsible for taking care of ourselves, which also means knowing when to back off from something that is doing more harm than good. Benefits should outweigh the consequences, not the other way around. We are not intended to torture ourselves."

A few weeks after stopping the injections, a new symptom developed. I felt intense pain in my skin, as if someone were forcing my arms through a meat grinder until they were completely raw, and then soaking them in an acid bath. This situation was compounded by searing pains in both of my legs, from my knees down. I was in agony both with and without the medicine.

Without a doubt, I knew something was wrong with me and no medication seemed to alleviate my suffering. It was not fair. I wanted to know what was causing this, and I asked anyone who would listen. Unfortunately, this left me open to judgment from others who misconstrued my meaning. I was astonished at the number of Christians who felt they needed to inform me that my symptoms were punishment from God for something I had done in my life.

The sheer number of people who shared their scriptural ignorance further compounded my anger with God. Nothing in the Bible says God will punish someone in this way for having done something wrong. Separate from "scriptural discipline," as others called it, I know there are natural consequences in life. An example would be the potential that the extremely high temperature I had as a teenager could have triggered the MS.

Regardless of my perceived anger with God, there came a time when I wanted to be close to Him. I needed His protection and comfort. After endlessly searching, we found an amazing Vineyard church. The pastor there, Ray Hollenbach, selflessly spent hours praying with me. He was my next silver lining, the pastor who helped me get back on track. Through his time and prayers, my heart's view returned to God. Again I reminisced of His promise to me for a life of many years.

I could not go through life feeling the way I was with such a hard bitter heart brought on by intense pain and frustration from the MS. What could I do to make it better? I turned my attention back to God, academic classwork, and doing what I could to heal. The first major change I made affected not only me, but also my entire family. I altered our diet, so we all made healthier and more nutritious food choices. With God back in the forefront of my life, I was able to move forward in spite of persistent neurologic symptoms.

During the fall of 2004, winter arrived with a vengeance—and very low temperatures. The intense pain in my skin returned. I was uncomfortable wearing clothes or having anything touch my skin, including the blankets on my bed. Physically, it became difficult for me to walk from my car to the buildings at school. After walking a distance of about fifty feet in the cold, I could not grasp an exterior doorknob at the school to get into the building. Chip and I discussed the issues I was having and agreed that my symptoms seemed more incapacitating in the cold than the warm weather of the south. We decided it was time to return to Florida.

My expected graduation date was spring of 2005 and I wanted to stay in Kentucky long enough to walk at my undergraduate commencement exercises. In the face of all life's potholes, I felt my attendance was a paramount milestone. How awesome would it be for my kids to know about my trials and then watch me successfully complete my degree?

During my final spring term, I started round two of my research. God blessed me with far more results during this round than those from the prior year. In fact, at the project's conclusion, I had thousands of living lamprey larvae that I returned to the location where I had collected the adults. Then I made plans to start working towards getting the research published.

In the weeks following graduation, we packed ourselves and moved back to Florida, where Chip went back to work for his former employer at Kennedy Space Center. I am so grateful for my time in Kentucky, even with all the trials. It was through those difficulties that I believe I learned to talk regularly with God. I trusted that He was there and I gave Him credit for every accomplishment. You could say this is when I started to acknowledge His presence in my everyday life.

When we first arrived back in Florida during the summer of 2005, we decided to rent a home so we could take the necessary time searching for our ideal "forever home". We were not having much luck until one day when I was out driving around and felt led into an unfamiliar area. There, I found a new-construction neighborhood that appeared to be clean and quiet, yet close to amenities. That afternoon, I took Chip to see it. With his approval, we signed a contract to have our house built. Yes, we did this at the peak of the economic bubble.

Since we chose to have our house built from the ground up, we wanted to make sure it was built on a solid spiritual ground. To do this, we met with our pastor before the construction company broke ground. He came to our lot, and as a family, we anointed the land with oil and the kids buried a cross in the back yard.

During the building process, we met with friends at the construction site to pray together over the hands that were building our house. We asked for the Lord's favor. For added blessing, we requested that the builders pour the concrete foundation over a Bible. Once the walls were up, but before drywall was installed, we wrote scriptures on the concrete blocks above or below every door and window.

During March of 2006, while we were in the rental property, Chip received orders back to active duty with the military. His expected ship-out date was not until the fall, so he was home to help us move into our new home in May. By August of 2006, I noticed potential neurologic symptoms developing once again. However, I was so excited about being in my new house and getting it organized that I decided to ignore the warning signs and hoped they would go away.

In the months before we moved into our new construction home, I prayed that God would send us to the perfect church family. He was quick to respond. For two weeks, as I daily drove past Indian River City United Methodist Church[2], I felt as if I had been hit in the head with a two-by-four. I realized that was God's way of telling me we should join this church.

We attended the church only twice before my neurologic symptoms became too obvious to hide. Regardless, I tried to ignore them because Chip was on active duty orders, so he couldn't help me. Besides, I believed the symptoms would go away if I stopped thinking about them. Worst case, I told myself, maybe it was just anxiety over Chip's deployment—and that was something I could handle. I was wrong. Our Family's darkest days were upon us.

---

[2] Location of this church is in appendix B.

PHOEBE A Walker

Chapter 6

Life's pivot point

My neurologic symptoms continued to spiral out of control until *THE* day that changed everything. It was the fall school term of 2006, when I was thirty-three years old. After both of my kids left for school, my type "A" personality and I were in the bathroom getting ready for another full day. But, when I stepped out of the shower, I dropped to the floor like a ton of bricks. This was going to be a very different kind of day, I realized immediately.

I tried to push myself up, but realized I was not moving. Then I looked around to see what was preventing my movement, as if something could physically restrain me without my noticing. I realized I was literally stuck on the floor and confused because nothing visible was restraining me.

I stopped struggling for a moment and felt my heart sink as I attempted to process what was happening. "God," I asked, "what is this? What is happening to me—and how long will it last? How am I supposed to respond? How can I get up?" After forcing myself back into the moment, I realized I needed help. Immediately. There was no time for fear, anger, pity, or tears. I just needed to act.

Whom could I call? We had just moved into the new construction neighborhood, and I had no neighbors on our road. Chip! I needed to call him.

It took me about thirty minutes to move the twelve feet from one side of the bathroom to the other, where my phone was. My movement was peculiar, a combination of scooting, crawling, and rolling. I could not control my appendages. It was around nine o'clock when I finally managed to contact Chip. I apologized profusely that this was happening, but I really needed him. Could he help? "Please, Lord," I prayed, "let him be able to help."

Chip told me that he could hear the fear in my voice. He immediately sought emergency leave. After the call, it took me an additional hour and a half to get myself dressed because I could not functionally use my arms or legs. A two-year-old could dress himself or herself with better ease than I could.

The dog's bark alerted me to Chip's arrival at home, about eleven-thirty that morning. I knew I needed to be closer to the door before he came in. I believed that if I were in the right place, the severity of my situation would not be so apparent. Now I am not sure where my logic was at the time, but I honestly believed I could hide my symptoms enough to help reduce Chip's fear. After all, he was leaving the country in three weeks; he did not need to worry about this.

Chip opened the front door before I got into the "right place." His first glimpse of me was mortifying. My attempt to walk down the hallway was not so much walking. What he saw were four pieces of human spaghetti slopping against the walls and floor. I could feel my legs wobbling under me, and my arms did little more than prevent my head from smashing into walls.

It is difficult for me to give a clear picture of what Chip saw because I was not able to observe it for myself. At best, I know what I felt like, and the expression in his eyes completed the story. Chip stopped in the doorway with a bag on each shoulder and one in each hand. I saw tears well up in his eyes and his jaw drop as his bags simultaneously fell to the floor. What? Didn't he see my HUGE smile, the one I carried on my face down the hall? It had taken a great amount of energy to put it on my face and not cry it off the moment he walked in the front door. I guess no smile was big enough to cover the fact that I had no control over my body.

That was the first time in our marriage that I saw fear in my husband's eyes. His expression painted a painfully vivid picture of the situation. I did not want him to be scared because I was already mortified enough for the two of us.

Somehow, with Chip at home, I knew God was near, even though I could not see him. Now it was time to get me to the church and that is exactly what Chip did. He took me to the church we had visited only twice. There I met with God at the altar. Because I was so overwhelmed, I could not find the words to pray.

"Please read my heart Father for what I am trying to say," I prayed.

After deciding to write this book, I asked Chip what went through his mind that day he stood in the doorway. This is what he said:

> *"My initial thought, when I saw you, was complete horror. I think my heart dropped into my stomach, not so much about me personally, but about you. I wondered what was causing this. I thought, how could I help you? How are we going to get through*

this? Did I do something to cause this? What could I have done differently?

Then I told myself we just had to get through the moment. I needed to figure out how I could I help her. What can we do to fix this? Can we fix this? My wife is broken, and I can't fix her. How do I help her? God I love her. What about our kids, where are they?

I thought that I needed to get her to the hospital. I was upset that I could not get home sooner. I asked myself how my family would manage. I remember thinking that the kids were going to need to help Gretchen a lot more. Can they? Will they? Will she be able to walk again? Will she need a wheelchair for the rest of her life?"

I figured those and many other thoughts and worries would be crossing his mind. It did not matter how desperately I tried to minimize his perceived severity of the situation, I could see in his eyes that he felt it anyway. Regardless, I attempted again to play it off as anxiety over his deployment. I told him after I adjusted to his departure, everything would return to normal. We told ourselves that my symptoms might begin to settle down with him at home for two weeks on emergency leave.

We were wrong!

Eating became difficult for me because I could not hold eating utensils. During his first night home, Chip made me a plate of food and brought it to me with utensils. This was not unusual; he had done this for years. Yet on this night, I remember crying because he brought me utensils that I could not hold and he served me mashed potatoes and peas.

I wondered how I could eat that food with utensils that I couldn't hold. Eventually I swallowed my pride, scooped some mashed potatoes with my hands, smashed them into the peas, and then shoveled the mess into my mouth. It did not take long for Chip to realize what he had done. After apologizing and shedding a few tears, he took my plate and prepared finger foods for me.

The second week Chip was home, my eyes became the center of attention. First, they wouldn't stop itching. The next day they were still irritating me and my vision became blurred. As Chip's emergency leave was about to expire, my vision became much worse. However, even with the obstruction in my sight, I still had functional vision. I figured the cause of this obstruction was stress over Chip's upcoming deployment and I continued to ignore it.

During the next two days, my peripheral vision completely diminished. On the third day, my physical abilities to do things for myself were severely impaired, to the point that I required a trip to the Emergency Room.

The Emergency Room doctor determined that I was suffering from "something neurologic," and gave me a steroid shot, hoping that the steroid would prevent my symptoms from getting worse. This offered minimal temporary relief. The doctor sent me home with a referral to a neurologist for follow-up treatment.

The next day, Monday, Chip drove me to see the neurologist we were referred to, who ordered intravenous steroids for three days.

The doctor arranged for home health administration of the medications to begin in two days. The same day Chip returned to his duty station.

A nurse came to my home to administer the IV, but she had difficulties getting the needle into my arm. She stuck me seven times without success. One of her attempts caused me to bleed, leaving a puddle of blood on the floor the diameter of a Ritz cracker.

Even with limited vision, I remember the look of horror on Ashley's face as she walked in the front door after school and saw the nurse sticking me. She saw my blood all over the table and floor. I became frustrated that the woman kept trying when she was so ineffectual in hitting a vein. We exchanged words over her determination to stay and complete her work and my desire to avoid more pain and preserve my blood. Without having the IV started, I cut off the argument when I firmly told her, "You are done. Now get out of my house … please!"

Yet I still needed to take the medication. How was I going to handle that? I had to find someone capable of starting an IV. My initial thought was the hospital. I contacted Vicki, the mother of one of Ashley's friends, who was a nurse there. She agreed to take me. The hospital could not use the IV medication I brought from my house for safety reasons. However, they were able to obtain a new order from the neurologist. The order called for me to go back to the hospital every twenty-four hours for administration of medication. Vicki took me the first night, a person I vaguely knew from the church took me the next night, and my mother-in-law took me the last night.

I felt like I was walking in the shadow of death every time someone insisted that tomorrow would be a better day. It was such a horrible thing to hear as I watched every day get worse for months without a break. I was so glad for one of Pastor Jim Govatos' sermons when he addressed the scriptural meaning of "a better tomorrow." My heart melted in confirmation and relief that someone understood my situation. He explained that "scriptural tomorrow" oftentimes refers to the end of the trial, however long that takes. Sometimes it can literally mean tomorrow, but most often, the time is substantially longer. In my case, it seemed never-ending. As one symptom improved, two new symptoms developed in its place. Jim became my next silver lining. I found hope in the messages he taught.

Add pain that changed daily and further deterioration of my vision to the existing issues with my hands and walking. I could no longer do anything for myself and became blind in both eyes, seeing only blackness. I was an invalid who could not perform simple activities of daily living, like clothing, feeding, or cleaning myself. I could not get myself to the bathroom, open doors, or turn light switches on and off; I became a useless blob on the floor. With everything I was experiencing, I never asked God why, because I was sure there was a reason. Instead, I gave Him an earful of my anger because I was uncomfortable and scared. I could not feel Him near me. I cried for Him to come, desperately needing Him to hold me and make everything okay.

In hindsight, I realized I never saw Him because he was super close. Just like when you take the palm of your hand and move it towards your face until it touches your nose. If you did not know it was your hand, you would not be able to recognize it. That is how close I believe God was during that time.

⌒⌒⌒⌒⌒

Ashley was in elementary school, the first to leave in the morning and return in the afternoon. When my eight-year-old came home from school, she felt responsible for helping me. This included taking me to my bathroom to clean me—of urine, feces, and, for four days, the added mess of menses. I still shed tears when thinking about what that little girl had to endure in order to help her mother, at that age. No child should ever have to grow up that fast. I knew my life was not fair, then I looked at what she was doing for me and it crushed my heart. I blamed myself for the life she was enduring. Thankfully, God blessed her heart because she just wanted to do whatever she needed to for her mom. She tells me she doesn't remember the worst of it.

When I ask her to reflect on what she saw and how she felt, this is what she said:

> *At first, I was not only thinking about but also hoping that she would get better. But as time wore on, Momma only got worse and worse. I started to realize, at eight years old, I could lose my mom forever. We had not gotten to do many mother-daughter things yet. I tried to do anything I could, hoping that little things would help her get better. When I felt like I was going to cry, I would leave the area where she was and go cry in my room or anywhere else I thought she would not hear me. I felt like I had to be strong for her and do what she*

couldn't, but being eight years old, there wasn't much I could do for her.

I felt useless and was always worrying, but did not want to say it. Time drew onward to get worse before it got better. When it got as bad as it would get, I almost lost hope in Mom getting better. At the worst of this, at church, I went to the kneeling rail by myself and asked God to save my mother. Then Mom slowly started to get better, and I gained hope that she would live and be able to be there for me in the future when I needed her the most.

Even with hope returning to me, I was still eight years old and so dreadfully afraid something would change again and turn for the worst and I would never see her again. If something had happened to her, I do not know what would have happened to me. She was my path to Christ, and without a path, I could stray from what was right into a sinful life.

Things continued to get better and I worried less and less but, even to this day, I have not stopped worrying that out of nowhere it could happen again. When the worry gets too big, I have to remember to step back, take a deep breath and pray to our dear sweet Lord to keep my momma safe and in his loving hands.

Because I had become a blind invalid with two young children in the home and no regular help, my husband's commanding officer told him he was not going to deploy; his commander could not send Chip away with our current situation. Instead, he found two other individuals to take his orders, in this way neither one had to take on the full set alone. (I send a special thank you to those who took Chip's place!!!) These two individuals were priceless silver linings. I have no words to express my gratitude for the sacrifice those two men made. Because of them, I did not have to be alone in my darkness. Chip was allowed to remain in close proximity.

Chip was still on active duty orders and instructed to remain with his command until the orders expired. He continued to make road trips several hours each, one way, twice a day, several days a week. This made it possible for him to get me to my medical appointments and for him to help because I could do nothing for anyone, not even myself. In total, it was three months before Chip was able to transfer his military work location. At the new location, he was close enough to our house that he could comfortably commute daily. He continued this way until the end of his orders in March 2007.

It became apparent that we needed to research this MS and learn as much as we could about it. I needed to identify what things made it worse and what things lessened the severity of my symptoms. We clearly needed direction in how to move forward. The next chapter shares much of what we learned about this disease.

Chapter 7
What is MS Anyway?

Chip had to carry me into the office the first day I met my new neurologist in the fall 2006. I could not walk, much of my vision was gone, and I did not have a wheel chair. The doctor ordered a brain MRI to see what changes were present. The MRI revealed that I had more than 75 lesions between my brain and my spine, many of them still active. These confirmed our fears. The doctor diagnosed me with Multiple Sclerosis—the third time I had heard those words from doctors.

This time I was not shocked and I did not fight it. I just wanted to live. I was ready to accept the diagnosis and learn to live with it. I was prepared to dance in a hurricane, which I continue doing today.

We all have white blood cells that help fight infection. In normal people, when the infection is defeated, the white blood cells park themselves until they have another bug to go fight. In a person with multiple sclerosis, however, the white blood cells do not stop their work; they continue to chew away at tissue, even though it is healthy tissue. The medical world calls these sites lesions, holes in the protective covering of a nerve. This creates a disconnection in the message that goes from the brain to each respective body part.

To address my blindness, the neurologist sent me to a neuro-ophthalmologist. That specialist confirmed that I was suffering from optic neuritis, swelling of the optic nerve. This is one of the key symptoms in MS, and the reason I had become black blind.

I explain to people that a lesion is similar to the wire on a lamp, or any other electronic device. When the wire is void of the rubber outer edge, sometimes the device turns on, sometimes it does not, and yet other times the device will flicker between off and on. This phenomenon continues to worsen the longer the devise is on because the exposed wire gets hot. The electrical messages are not completely relayed, which prevents the device from functioning properly. That same response happens with the nerves in a person with MS. Sometimes we function okay, and sometimes we do not, while other times we are just flat out unsure of what to expect.

I have discovered that environmental climates affect my abilities as well. Going back to the wire example, if it gets too hot or cold, then symptoms are exacerbated. Some people with MS can tolerate cold better than hot, while others find the reverse is true for them. However, for most people with MS, I believe the complication most likely comes from a variation of extreme temperatures.

We can suffer from difficulties walking, swallowing, or speech. We may experience a prickly or burning sensation in the skin, vision disturbances or complete loss of sight, spasticity, incontinence, pain, and a plethora of other symptoms. Some are treatable, but generally only with medications that come with their own side effects. I tend to "just walk" through the symptoms without the medications, because I think the side effects are far worse.

The drive to the neuro-ophthalmologist's office seemed never-ending, because I could not see where we were or if we were almost there. This was the longest distance I had ridden in a car without my sight, which may have contributed to my elevated anxiety. I kept asking Chip if we were close and if not, how much time remained. He said I reminded him of a child asking, "Are we there yet? ... Are we there yet?" He said it was cute. He made it his job to try to keep a smile on my face, but maybe it was to help put a smile on his face, too. When I was not thinking about where we were in route, I was wondering if the doctor was going to tell me I would be blind forever.

It is amazing that after having sight for thirty-three years, I never realized the full extent of its influence in my daily life. Without vision, I had no concept of time, which made even the infinitesimal things seem to take forever. As an artist and painter, I found that one of the most difficult side effects was the loss of color. No matter how hard I tried, I could not visualize color or shapes. Everything was just black—not levels or variations of black, but the darkest black I have ever experienced. It was disconcerting, unnerving, even frightening never knowing who was near me, where I was, and what people were doing around me.

While I waited to see the doctor, thoughts swirled around in my head. I kept thinking there was a real possibility that my sight would never return. I even questioned whether it was part of MS, because I had been told that optic neuritis was only supposed to affect one eye at a time. Yet I had no vision in either of my eyes.

The moment of truth came as I was sitting in the exam chair and the doctor asked if I could see how many fingers he was holding up. Swallowing my fear, I somberly replied, "I can't see anything." Then I heard clinking around and the doctor explain that he was going to look into my eyes with a very bright light. Hope! There was hope for a minute because this is what I had been waiting for.

In the past, this light had been painfully bright. Surely, I thought, I would at least be able to see a hint of light. With his hand on my forehead, I began to *will* myself to see the light. After what seemed like quite a bit of time had passed and I had not seen anything, I asked, "Is the light on yet?"

The three people in the room replied with unilateral confirmation, "YES!" **BAM!** My world broke in two. Darkness and devastation covered me and imbedded an inexplicable level of fear. I found myself swallowing. Hard. I could hear my loud gulp as I pondered how I was going to live as a blind person.

"We need some baseline tests," the doctor told Chip and me. He sent me for a visual field test. Here they put the patient's head in a dome-shaped machine, cover one eye, and place a clicker in the patient's hand. In the dome, the patient faces straight ahead. As lights appear, the patient clicks the button. In this way, the doctor can identify the individual's field of vision.

I could not tell whether I was looking straight ahead or not and think I even asked the technician if I was. After sitting in these tests before, I knew what to expect. It was so frustrating that I could not see any of the lights, that I actually contemplated pushing the clicker just because. As I listened to the "poor-me" fit developing, I heard sniffles coming from behind me. My heart dropped to the floor.

I was broken, and Chip could see it. Now he was sobbing because he knew he could not fix me. I did not want to be blind. How could I be his partner if I couldn't see? I felt as if I had just become a huge burden to this very hard-working and loving man. The situation was already overwhelming to me, now I could hear that it was for him, too.

The doctor's final comment on the issue gave me a smidge of relief: he confirmed that he believed my blindness was due to MS. "We'll just have to play the waiting game and hope for the best," he said, patting me on the arm. "If the vision loss is caused by the MS, that means it is most likely temporary."

Through this concept, I put my spiritual eyes on God and fully trusted that he would carry me through my latest trial. The question became how long will I have to wait? It was time to just believe and have faith while continuing to live.

PHOEBE A Walker

Chapter 8

The servants

In October of 2006, I was completely blind, my husband was away from home four or five nights out of the week, we didn't know many people, and I had two young children in my home. Our house was in a new neighborhood in Titusville, Florida, with no other homes completed on my road. How was I going to take care of my kids if I could not even take care of myself? I worried that the state was going to take my children from me.

At that time, TJ was in middle school. He was last to leave in the morning and to return home after school. On school days, before he left, I would sit on a couch in the front room, with one dog on either side of me like little cherubs. I remained there until either I slid myself to the floor or my daughter returned in the afternoon.

Six very long hours stretched between the time when TJ left in the morning and Ashley came home in the afternoon. During those hours, I constantly prayed that God would heal me and make things okay. Many times, I just sat and cried, especially after going to the bathroom on myself. This humiliation led to a new level of depression. I mocked myself for being a baby and commented that maybe someone should buy me diapers; it would make everyone's job easier. No matter how deep I dug within my soul, I found no nice words to say to myself.

Additionally, I refused to talk to others because I did not feel worthy. I felt dirty.

As the time neared for Ashley to arrive home, I remember feeling dread for what she would see when she walked through the door. The circumstances were completely unfair for my young daughter to endure. I didn't want to eat or drink because I wanted to reduce my waste. The Lord knows, I did not want this for her, but I was helpless to make any changes. Fortunately, her heart was strong enough to handle it. She has always been a silver lining in my life—and I was acutely aware of her sacrifices at this time.

Of everyone in my family, I was most concerned about my son. He was openly angry about my situation, and I could not help him. This was evident on several occasions. For instance, when I went into the kitchen, he would trap me in my wheelchair between objects. Around the island, he often placed a bag of garbage behind me and the trashcan in front of me, and then he left the room. I remained trapped until someone came to move the barricades; most of the time, that was Ashley.

At the time, TJ was too angry to articulate how he felt. He was in middle school and seemed to hate being there. He always came home angry, never did his schoolwork, and did not want to talk about the causes of his anger. Several years later, he told me it was because he always had bad days at school and then came home to a sick mother. He said he had not paid enough attention in science class to the lessons on cancer and he thought MS was like having cancer. This hurt his understanding of the differences between cancer and multiple sclerosis when he tried to compare the two. If I had known he was comparing the two, I might have been able to help him understand they were not the same.

Most of what TJ remembers about those days was that my condition continued to get worse, to the point where we needed help from others because our family was not here. When my condition did not get better, he said, "I was afraid that my mom might die." This caused many feelings to overwhelm him. He couldn't control what was happening and the combination of feelings confused him. Fortunately, a time came, months later, where he realized things were starting to get better.

Of course, I would have done anything to prevent this hurt that caused so much confusion and pain for my son. He may have lashed out at me in anger during this time, but I understand it was only because he was hurt and didn't know how to articulate his feelings. Unfortunately, he still has very conflicting feelings when it comes to me. I believe that one day he will find peace and we will be okay.

One day in the fall of 2006, I received a phone call from a woman at the church we had just started to attend. She explained that she knew we were in the middle of a difficult life situation and asked if she could help. I wondered how she knew we were having issues because I had not told anyone. Regardless, that call was a blessing from God. At first, pride got in the way as I started thinking, "How can I let anyone help me? What will they think of me after I let them close enough to see everything about me?" Then my mind shifted to the kids. I knew we desperately needed the help, so I told her I would be grateful to receive their assistance.

The caller was a member of a discipleship group. Our church had several running simultaneously. This woman made contact with every discipleship group and arranged dinners for four nights a week, which continued for about three months. An attorney at the church offered to help with legal disability benefits (which had continually denied me). Other people offered to help with my kids, especially when they needed to be picked up from school. Once, a women's group came to clean my house. Every person who came to our home lifted us up in prayer.

Of those who came to me, one of the most amazing people was Leanne. She just sat with me. I wondered how she could feel comfortable just sitting there in the dark, my darkness, and expect little to no conversation for hours? I love this angel for the sacrifice she offered; she made me feel priceless. It is the kind of love many do not know how to express, but unconditional love is the greatest blessing to receive. I welcomed anyone willing to join me in my darkness.

One of the most important connections was with the Order of St. Luke (OSL) healing prayer ministry. I vividly remember the first day we went for healing. Chip and I were the first to arrive, which allowed us to meet people as they came in. When it was time to go, everyone in the room stood in shock as they watched us leave. They did not know I had issues walking until they saw Chip throw me over his shoulder to carry me out of the church. To this day, I hear it recounted this way: "When we walked in the room, we were excited to see new people. We didn't know anything was wrong until Chip picked you up and threw you over his shoulder like a sack of potatoes when you left.

Then we knew why you were there." During this time without a wheelchair, Chip was my legs.

I found one of my deepest connections within OSL was a dear woman named Jo. At the time, she was the one who led the group. I believe our paths crossed as a direct response to my prayers. To this day, God continues to speak to me through her. Since then, I have come to realize that my connection was with the entire OSL prayer warrior team, whose members laid hands on me during this time of healing. When they anointed my head with oil and laid hands on me, I felt a divine power flow through my body, touching every cell and the spaces in between. At one of the weekly meetings, I learned about daily communion as a part of healing. For months, Chip and I integrated this into part of our daily prayer walk.

Surprisingly, the most difficult part of letting people help us was the picture they revealed to me of our situation. While they never actually told me, I could hear it in their voices and sniffling noses. I knew they were sobbing because of my situation.

As a Christian, I know we are to rejoice when our Christian family rejoices and mourn when they mourn. However, I did not want them to feel my brokenness; the Lord knows I felt it enough for all of us. I wish I could have given them something in which they could rejoice, because I do not like being the source of people's pain and discontent. Looking back, I feel fortunate to have had that many people who cared deeply enough to share so much of my pain.

During the healing process, countless total strangers stepped up to help us, overwhelming me with a depth of love I had never received before. This love manifested itself into a truly beautiful picture. It was a picture of angels pouring in through the woodwork behind me while I sat on the couch. I remember saying to myself, "I have so many people praying for me, even people who don't know me. I don't need to pray for my healing anymore."

Though I felt relief come with these wonderful people, I was still too uncomfortable in my condition to sleep much. During those sleepless hours, I prayed for everyone who was praying for me and whoever else came into my mind, even people from my past as far back as I could remember. For a while, I felt like I had gone down memory lane and connected with friends as far back as pre-school and middle school. To me, all of these people represented individual silver linings, rays of hope that projected me forward. It felt good not to pray for my healing anymore—and that is when I noticed things really started changing for the positive. Even better was the realization in days and weeks that followed, that God was showing up in even more profound ways.

Chapter 9

Encounter with an Angel

After nearly four months, healing was taking place, although I was still not well enough to take care of myself. I desperately wanted to be present for my kids in a positive way throughout their daily lives. During the Christmas season, TJ had a band concert at school, and that became a special moment during a bleak time. Chip was home, so he packed my wheelchair, the kids, and me into the truck and we went to the school together. It was like a breath of fresh air to get out of the house for something other than doctor's offices and church.

My positive outlook changed, however, soon after we arrived at the school. I felt like I was an embarrassment to TJ, and I felt smothered as people crowded around me. With minimal vision, the room sounded like Grand Central Station in the middle of a weekday. After months of living in quiet and darkness, the sensation made me very dizzy. The conversations taking place around me filled my head with a million thoughts that I could not stop. Why didn't I think about these possibilities before I opted to go out of the house?

When I was a child, I was very shy, but after I moved in with my dad, I worked to develop myself into a social butterfly. My need to get out and be social must have been too much to handle that night.

Couple that with how strongly I wanted to be present as a mother for my child. Those two desires were so strong that they caused me to overrule any thoughts that this might be too much stimulation too soon.

Each student had one parent sit next to him or her as the student played in the concert. I wanted to be that parent for TJ, but I couldn't because of the wheelchair. Of course, that spun me into a pity party mode. What compounded the issue was that I could not visually focus on any one thing. Because so much was going on around me, I opted to stare at the floor. I felt isolated and vulnerable because Chip was sitting with TJ and Ashley went off to find her friends. I sat alone while people walked around me as if I were a fixture on the floor.

When it was time to leave, Chip tried pushing my wheelchair out of the building, but the people in the crowd seemed intentional in racing to get in front of us and then stopping to chat with others. Chip got frustrated and started shouting in his military lingo, "Make a hole," while forcing my wheelchair through the crowd like a plow. Again, I thought how embarrassing that must have been for TJ. I wanted all of this to go away. Repeatedly, I wondered, "What am I doing to my family?"

As my vision started to come back, I remember thinking I saw something move in my extreme peripheral vision. I decided to experiment by reaching my right arm over my head and wiggling my fingers. YES! I could see them! Oh my goodness, the excitement when I realized there was correlation between my hand gestures and when I thought I saw something moving. I could not tell what I was seeing, but when I wiggled my fingers, I could see shadows moving. This activity evoked the same response in both eyes.

Rejoicing that I was no longer in solid blackness, I constantly did the "wiggle my fingers over my head" to remind myself that at least I had some semblance of vision. Upon experimentation in different lighting, I learned that when there was light, I could not see as well as when it was darker. I am sure my actions annoyed a few people. In fact, I remember them asking what I was doing. One person actually said it was annoying and would I please cease and desist.

Although I could see something, I was still legally blind. Regardless, I felt like life was good. Every day for weeks, I noticed sporadic spots appear in my vision. Each one was like a single piece of a puzzle and I was waiting for a bazillion more to complete the picture. Though there was improvement, my vision remained compromised by the inability to see lights or color, large holes remained in my vision, and I had no perception of depth. These limitations were frustrating and I began getting impatient with them. I started asking God whether this was it, the new me, or if I could bargain with him to have more vision restored.

My hope began to waver. The only way to obtain new hope in such a dismal time was in the Lord. I sat on the floor and started singing "Amazing Grace." Then I planted my face in the ground as I prayed to God and searched for one conceptual living blade of thriving grass to pierce through my floor. I knew I would not find a literal blade of grass growing through my carpet; but I was desperately seeking the hope of Christ.

In my search for hope, something swept over me. Was it the Holy Spirit? Then I heard my quivering voice say, "Father, as long as my blindness and inabilities are going to somehow better Your Kingdom, then I am willing to stay this way as long as it is necessary." "Wow, did I really just say that," I asked myself.

I felt the conviction to sing again, and I did. I sang "Amazing Grace" with as much intensity and emotion as I could muster. Time seemed to stand still, and then I felt drawn to look up to the sky where I received a divine peace that immersed deep within my core. In that moment, I felt endowed with answers to questions I did not know I had. I am sure this sounds confusing – it was for me, too. Though I was confused, I understood that everything was going to be okay, and that my condition was not going to be permanent. Regardless to this call for sacrifice, I sent up praises of thanksgiving that it was His plan to restore me.

Then, out of nowhere, about four feet from where I sat on the floor, I saw the most beautiful blue silhouette of an adult-sized human shape sitting in a chair. It was void of features. How could I see it? I had not been able to see light or color, yet I saw this color and it was glowing. Strangely, I felt compelled to talk to it. "I don't know who or what you are," I said. "Though I do not believe you are Jesus, I believe you were sent by Him because I can feel your divine presence."

I never heard an audible word spoken.

I felt the need to close my eyes and hold on tight, because God was in control of this ride. I again sang "Amazing Grace" with as much energy and love as I could put into the song. As I sang, I felt an inexplicable amount of peace fill me. The knot in my stomach dissolved. I had no sense of time. I did not want the angel to go away, because with it came a peace and comfort that could only have come from Heaven. To this day, I feel choked up when I think of this experience.

I did not want to tell people about the angel for fear of what they would think. Even though I was certain of the peace that came over me, I was still a little uncertain of what I had seen. This left me feeling comfortable to talk about the experience with any authority. A few weeks later, my pastor, Pastor Jim Govatos, did a sermon on angels. It confirmed for me that angels do exist and that it was possible that I really did see what I thought I saw.

The sermon cautioned us about wanting to see life-sized angels or miracles because generally the size of the angel or miracle directly corresponds with the task the recipient is being charged to fulfill. EUREKA! That made sense to me. Being blind and an invalid was a tremendous calling. How wonderful it was that God sent an angel large enough to help carry that burden for me!

The visit from this angel completely changed my life. To this day, I believe that was the moment I received my spiritual baptism. From that experience forward, my physical condition seemed to restore at a more rapid rate. Unlike the first time I asked God into my heart, this experience changed my heart overnight. Things that once upset me no longer did. Every person is worthy of being forgiven and loved no matter how horrible the action. I could not believe I was saying things like that, but it was true. There is no room for lack of forgiveness and love, no matter how difficult they are to achieve.

My life became about total humility, which I believe is the absolute foundation of following Christ. Additionally, I realized that

God allows our hardships so that we can help others through similar situations. He does this by taking our painful broken pieces and making them beautiful, in order to better the kingdom--which means that I had developed the potential to be someone else's silver lining. From this epiphany, I started referring to my MS as a blessing from God, not a curse. However, I still ask him to remove this thorn from my flesh; no part of it is desirable.

Chapter 10
Healing Takes Place

About a month into my blindness, in September 2006, Kachina Laymon, came to live with us. She was my next silver lining. I met her while I was a student at Campbellsville University in Campbellsville, Kentucky, between 2002 and 2005. When she came to our house, she brought her baby girl with her. It was a financial obligation we were not equipped to help her with, so she got a job to carry that weight. This new job significantly limited the time she had available to assist us, but we were so appreciative of the time she was available.

We still joke around about how much help she truly was, but honestly, the humor she levied on us brought levels of healing for everyone. One night, on a weekend when Chip was home, we went out for dinner at Sonny's restaurant. I could walk, but I was still legally blind. Kachina wanted to help me by being my guide person; she called herself my seeing-eye dog. She walked me into almost everything—people, chairs, and the buffet, as she escorted me to my seat.

I thought I was safe when we left the restaurant and were heading to the truck. The walk was smooth, and we successfully cleared the exit doors without incident. I was confident we were going to get to the truck without a situation when BAM. I knew I had just run into something solid and I could hear ringing in my ears. I shouted in laughter, "What in the world? Where did that come from?" Yep, Kachina had run me clean into the pole of a disabled sign in the parking lot.

Was this woman doing it on purpose? No, Kachina is not that kind of person – though she has more than her fair share of moments like this. I'm sure God allowed it for some much needed comedy relief. Everyone laughed so hard, it had to be cleansing to the soul.

The first place I go to meet with God is the altar at a church. There, I feel like I am sitting at the kitchen table with my "Abba" daddy, where we can talk and share thoughts. The second location I go to meet with God is the ocean. I attribute a great amount of my healing to the peace I absorbed while in God's presence on the beach. I go there to feel his physical touch, to feel his full embrace. When I was at my worst, I had someone guide me to both places.

One of my most amazing connections with God took place on an evening at the beach with Kachina. When we arrived at the beach, she helped me hobble to the spot where the waves met the dry sand. It was a moonlit evening and that lighting made it possible for me, with my limited vision, to see the white tips of the waves. They looked like God's fingertips, and that thought caused my heart to skip a beat as my eyes connected with them.

This was the first time I had been to the ocean since I had become blind and disabled which made it a truly special moment. I remember positioning myself where I could feel soggy wet sand on my feet—the kind that feels like quick sand sucking me in. This let me know that I was in the "Christ Touch Zone." I awaited the waves to come in.

Just as the water crashed into my shins, I cried out to the Lord for comfort and fell to my knees in the surf. As the current pulled out and the new waves crashed back on me, I felt like God was omnipresent, wrapping his arms around me. Like a loving parent, He was binding the fear and pain and dragging them far away.

When it was time to go home, we realized I was soaked to the bone and did not have a towel or dry clothes. That was okay because the pier where we parked was right next to Ron Jon's Surf Shop, which operates twenty-four hours a day. We decided to make a pit stop there to purchase dry clothes and a towel, so I could be more comfortable on the forty-five-minute trip back home.

The trip was memorable for another reason. Thanks to the outing, I slept better than I had in months. I cannot describe what a gift substantive sleep is after months where I couldn't sleep more than minutes to an hour at a time.

Another trip to the beach occurred one night after Kachina came home from work and realized I'd had a rough day. By that time, my sight was functional for getting around without running into things. I was able to hobble like a troll—at best, for mobility, but the day had not been an easy one. Kachina decided she would treat me to a trip to the beach so I could chat with God.

This gesture started as a good deed and ended with a legal repercussion. You see, when we reached the beach, she wanted to park as close to the walkway as she could so I would not have to walk too far. The problem was that she parked illegally in a no-parking zone. Darkness had already fallen outside and no one was around, what were the odds that a police officer would drive past? Call it our unlucky night. After our time on the beach, we returned to the truck to discover a ticket under the wiper blade.

But the problem did not stop there. I was still having physical issues with my hands, which prevented me from writing the check. This forced me to delay paying the ticket for a couple of weeks. After waiting as long as I could to write the check, I realized no matter how hard I tried, I could not *will* myself to do something that was physically impossible. I made multiple attempts to write something – anything. No matter how hard I tried, my fingers flat out refused to make anything that resembled a number or letter.

I finally conceded to my inability and asked Kachina to write the check for me. Then I scribbled nonsense for a signature and said, "Perfect. Now the bank will know for sure it came from me. Ha! Let's see how far it flies." After I mailed the check to the city, I decided I should probably contact the bank and explain that they would be getting a check with scribbles. "Please accept it," I asked. And they did.

The first day I was able feed myself, I ate at the dinner table, with utensils. When I finished eating, I got up, carefully pushed my chair in, grabbed my plate and silverware, and walked toward the sink. Every step was slow and carefully thought out, because my hands were occupied. I knew that if I fell, I would not be able to catch myself before hitting the floor. Chip turned around and was startled with what he saw. He wanted to reach out and take my dishes from me, but I smiled at him and said, "No! I want to do it by myself. Please let me." Then I added, "Look! I'm DOING it! ALL … BY … MYSELF!" I cried many tears from the pride I felt for this tremendous accomplishment. It was as if I had learned to walk for the first time.

My steps may have been slow and heavy, but I got where I was intending to go. This marked my first real contribution to cleaning up after myself since my MS episode started. I cannot remember the exact timing, but this occurred about five months after my initial neurologic symptoms.

Once my vision started returning at an accelerated rate, I remember thinking that I should draw a picture because people would be amazed with what I saw. However, I never got around to doing it. Initially, only one segment of my vision completely returned as a solid picture, and that was the extreme peripheral. I described my view as much like trying to see a full picture though a pinhole—but from the side, not the middle.

The center of my vision returned only one speck at a time. At first, it was easy to notice new specks because I started with a solid black background. Sporadic specks slowly appeared in no particular order or location. If you imagine a black-and-white picture covered with hundreds of holes scattered all over it, that is what some of my earlier full views resembled. Everything was black and white. I had no depth perception, and lots of missing pieces. Regardless of the choppy view, though, I celebrated every new piece of restored vision.

About six months after my first visit with the neuro-ophthalmologist, I had my first follow-up appointment. This one found me back in front of that dome for another visual field test. Chip and I were flipping through magazines to pass time while we waited to be called into the exam room. What a difference six months had made. I cannot describe how wonderful I felt this time because I could actually see again. Well … for the most part, I could.

One of the magazine advertisements showed a picture of grilled meat. I got excited and shouted "grilled chickie." Chip chuckled and said, "Nope, that's sausage." We came to another meat advertisement, I said, "Okay, I didn't get the last one but I've got this one – this one IS chickie – cluck cluck!"

My husband began laughing so hard he nearly fell out of his chair. "Nope," he said. "That's the same picture as the last one." When I flipped to the back page, there was yet another picture of grilled meat. I thought, maybe I should not guess on this one because I had missed the last two. However, I was so confident in my answer that I shouted, "This one is pig – oink oink." He said, "Nope, that's cow … moo." I guess, maybe my vision was not as good as I thought it was, but it sure provided a humorous moment. Now, the running joke is that I cannot keep my poultry, cows, and pigs straight. Apparently, to me they were all the same.

＊ ＊ ＊

When my vision returned enough for me to see objects and my physical abilities improved enough to allow me some independence, I began attempting to tackle chores. I walked around my house intentionally looking for something that I could do. When I found a small piece of lint or trash on the floor, I picked it up and threw it away. At last, I had found something I could do to help my family. While that activity level did not match my former level of family caretaker, as I had been from before the disability, it was a step in the right direction. No matter how mundane my accomplishments were, I gave praises to God for my increasing abilities.

＊ ＊ ＊

Before I lost my sight, I enjoyed carving surfboard shapes out of 36"x 12" rectangular pieces of wood. My intention was to shape, sand, and paint them, but I was in the middle of sanding three boards when the disability began. Though I could not paint the pictures on them without my eyesight, I realized I could sand them. There was no better time than loss of vision to start sanding because I did not need my eyes for this activity. In fact, I think my inability to see the boards made for a much smoother surface. I relied on my sense of touch, rather than eyesight, and they became the smoothest boards I have produced, to date.

Today one of the boards is hanging on my wall, I sold one on e-bay, and the other is at MaDD Jack's Grillin Shack restaurant in Cape Canaveral, Florida; voted the fourth best barbeque restaurant in the U.S. by Trip Advisor.[3] Not only was this craft something I could do, it was something that I can still tangibly touch from that time in my life. The boards serve as reminders of where I was and a vision of growth. During that somber time in my life, it was good to feel like I had some purpose, something to create when so much had been taken away. What is even better is that I still have access to two of them whenever I want.

Eventually I decided I had enough vision to attempt painting. I spent three weeks painting a design that under normal circumstances would have taken me only three hours to complete. The reason for the delay … without depth perception, I could not tell when the end of the paintbrush was touching the board, which was a serious challenge. I went through high levels of frustration and anger when the paint did not come off the brush onto the board, just to realize the brush was not even touching the surface. Other times, out of impatience, I over-compensated, by pressing the brush extra hard, leaving globs of paint on the board. Another issue was that I could only see gray scale, which created the need for assistance with paint colors.[4]

I was extremely excited and felt blessed to regain so many abilities, but I also had many frustrations over my desire to have more.

---

[3] Madd Jacks contact information is in appendix A.
[4] My website has photos of my paintings. Web address is in appendix A.

I realized, it did not matter how good I was at doing something or even my ability to accomplish it on my own, I should always be open and accepting of help from others.

Throughout the healing time, I regularly checked to see if my vision was good enough to move to the next step. It had been more than six months since I last drove. One day I thought my vision was restored enough to attempt this milestone. I wanted to start slowly, so I chose a short distance with straight roads and minimal traffic. Before climbing into the vehicle, though, I failed to take into consideration the overcast sky, which severely decreased my already limited vision. Remember also that I still could not see lights when I looked directly at them.

All was going well until I was driving down a road that required me to keep to the left in order to avoid the building traffic in the right lane. I slammed on the brakes, and I think my heart stopped beating. There had been an accident, and about forty feet in front of me was a police car with all its lights on. Yes, lights that I could not see because they became invisible when I looked directly at them.

I crept the vehicle forward to the spot where the police officer fervently gestured for me to stop – with his finger. I rolled my window down. "Didn't you see me here?" he demanded to know.

I realized that I needed to respond carefully. Out came "I do now. Yes, sir."

"You should have your eyes examined," he suggested, and sent me on my way.

As I drove off I thought, I guess it was a good thing I didn't tell him that I'd had my eyes examined the week before. He might have taken my license away on the spot. When I returned home, I conceded that it was entirely too soon for me to drive. I hung up my keys, for a bit longer and was grateful nothing worse had happened.

⁓

By the summer of 2007, about nine months after my initial onset of disabilities, nearly eighty percent of my vision had returned and I regained my abilities to do most things for myself. I believe God was the source behind this healing—it all started returning on its own several months before the doctors ever started me on regular three-times-a-week medicine.

Despite that significant level of healing, sometimes I could not control the force behind my body's actions. One day someone rang the doorbell and I tried to run from the back of the house to the front door before that person left. What actually happened went something like this: thud, step, smack, thud, step, smack. The leg I could not control landed where it wanted to, followed by the power of the good leg propelling me forward and consequently slamming me into the wall. I did this for a distance of about thirty feet.

Once I reached the front door and opened it, I could not stop myself. Out the front door I flew, looking for anything to halt my forward momentum. Ah, ha! There was a palm tree in the middle of the front yard. I reached my arm out like a hook. Yep, worked like a charm. It catapulted me straight at the front of the house. Forward I went, right through the flowerbed, where I took out the garden gnome and smacked into the wall at the doorbell. Okie dokie, I was now stopped, to the utter astonishment of my visitor. I decided I needed to make a mental note that next time I should attempt to approach the front door a bit more slowly.

Once I was no longer running around like a wild banshee, I could hear my surroundings. It was heavy laughter. The person who rang my doorbell was half standing, half falling against the wall, laughing and snorting so hard he was crying. No matter, he was entirely too amused by what he had just seen. He could do little more than hold his own gut from laughter.

A few weeks later, my comedy reel ran again. This time it began with the phone ringing. I ran toward the room to the left of the front door, taking the same path I had used previously, when I accidentally flew out the front door. This time my legs were doing much better, so the run was not an issue. However, I overshot where I was supposed to turn. Fortunately, I corrected my path just before I ran into the wall. This was only a minor detour. I simply went past the coffee table and turned to come back toward the corner next to the couch. As I turned to grab the phone, I lost my balance and flipped backwards over the arm of the couch. I landed folded in half, with my back on the wall and my butt on the floor. To add insult to injury, I was unsuccessful at answering the phone before the caller hung up.

Surely, I thought, in my failure to answer the phone in time, I should have at least earned some sort of reward for that perfect half-pike that took place over the edge of the couch. It was flawless! Kidding, of course, but those were the moments I wish I could have recorded to replay whenever I wanted some real time humor in the middle of my valley. Yes, having MS can bring very ugly days. But I have to tell you, I have found so much joy, love, and humor in my attempt to combat this disease. I *choose* to have more good days than bad, so I will continue to seek out the good and focus on the funny moments rather than the tragic ones.

Nowadays, whenever I start having an exacerbation of neurologic symptoms, my doctor orders a high dose of intravenous steroids, coordinated to work with my regular three-times-a-week injections. The IV medication reduces swelling of my nerves, which helps reduce the symptoms. When he orders the intravenous medication, I go to an infusion center to have it administered.

Comedy relief followed me to the infusion center, not only from my body's own malfunctioning, but also from that of the individuals who occupied my space. For instance, I think Chip was always trying to pay me back for something I didn't do. You see, there was something in the infusion center that triggered his fart gland. No kidding, every time we went, there was some sort of fart-a-thon coming from his tail end. To this day, I do not know what triggers it. This is perhaps God's way of lightening the mood – a divine wind.

On one of our visits to the infusion center, Chip started sniffing the air around him. I asked what he was doing. "Someone just farted near me," he said. That was, funny, because we were in a private room and no one was near us. Besides, I could not smell anything. Then he stood up and walked to the door to see if he could identify the source of the odor. Oh, my goodness, I think I was smacked in the face with a fart-nugget and the IV prevented me from moving fast enough to get away, so I just stayed down. "Chip – it burns!" I chuckled. My eyes were burning and my gut-wrenching laughter caused me dribble on myself. I was a hot mess.

One of my nurses, Sylvia, was in the room next door during the commotion. When she peeked around the corner, I told her that Chip was blaming someone else for his own flatulence. Unable to hold her own composure, she laughed and warned him, "You better not bring that out into the hallway. Just keep that in there."

Chip could not help himself. He wanted to share. From the door, he started jumping into the hallway and back into my room several times, just to stir the eau de fart scent into the hallway. I am not sure, but I think they had to call in a hazmat team to sanitize that space before they could bring in a new patient. I'm joking, of course, but really, days like this brought forth some of the best healing. Humor has definitely been one of God's silver linings for me.

All of this healing was wonderful and somewhat uplifting to see actual progress in my recovery. Having fun on the journey made the hard times tolerable. Now that restoration was about complete, it was time to start thinking about the next step for me. What would my new life look like?

PHOEBE A Walker

Chapter 11
A New Start

Before the entire MS thing railroaded me like a freight train in the fall of 2006, Chip was about to deploy overseas with the military, and we were actively preparing for his departure. This process included getting financial affairs in order, making sure we had all the accurate emergency contact information, up-to-date power of attorney and living wills, and contact information for military ombudsman.

As the spouse of a military member, whenever I knew he was going away, I intentionally planned things that would occupy my mind. It always helped our time apart to go much faster. This time I wanted the activity to be something fun that would occupy me for the entire duration of his deployment and culminate into something special for all of us on the other end. We were about to celebrate our ten-year anniversary, so I thought, "Let's do a vow renewal." However, we almost canceled it because of my physical struggles.

The months-long preparations for this ceremony were stored in boxes that got lost in a corner somewhere after the disease came and crushed me. Many months later, in the spring of 2007, I felt strong enough to ask myself, "Should I pull the boxes out and resume the preparations?"

Was I crazy to go ahead with this? I believed not.

The truth is, my life was drastically shaken to levels I did not know were livable. Then, like Bette Midler's song *Wind beneath My Wings*, I always turned behind me and knew Chip was standing there. He could have left at any point. Chip worked full time at a civilian job and full time at his military job in addition to running around full time with my medical needs and kids' schedules. To compound his schedule further, he continued to keep up with his own fitness by working out almost daily. I imagine that was part of how he coped with all he made himself responsible for.

Chip could have used his hectic life as an excuse to refuse to help me with any of the medical procedures I went through. He could have denied me the opportunities to move around looking for the right climate for the disease. Yes, he could have given up at any point along the way. But he did not. That man has a level of love for me that is difficult to find. I know God gave me the absolute best when he designed my husband to be my earthly partner. I wanted the world to know that, so I wrote my vows for the vow renewal service.[5]

This is what I wrote, "You are my best friend, with whom I share my dreams, play time, and prayer time. I share my everything with you. In you, I can see a breath-taking image of God's love for me. He was incredible in how he created only you for me, how you loved me endlessly when I could not even find myself. You tried to put my pieces back together to make me whole again. You've held my hand in the darkness and numbness to pull me back into the light of Christ. We have endured excessive trials together with great strength and victory

---

[5] The entire vow renewal ceremony is printed in Appendix C.

as God has intended. I love you with my entire soul, a place that only you and God may reside! Thank you for marrying me again. My vow to you is that I can give back to you all that you are and all that you have given me—and much more, with the help of God. I love you."

Yes, we needed to celebrate, and we needed to do it big. Okay, there were times I thought I was crazy because, though the timing was spot on, the workload was difficult. I did most of the preparations alone and easily tired from the process.

I asked Rana to be my matron of honor for this vow renewal. She and I had maintained a strong sisterly relationship over the years since we met in 1994, during my first marriage. Since the Justice of the Peace initially married Chip and I in March 1997, we asked Rana to be in our wedding ceremony in December of that year. Both she and Cristi were in our wedding party then. I am not sure why I did not also contact Cristi to be in this vow renewal service. It may be as simple as I asked people who were actively in contact with me during my incapacitated times, to be participants in the ceremony. With visual issues, I could not look up phone numbers. Regardless, Rana became my matron of honor and planned an extended stay to my house of three weeks. She flew in from Ohio and helped me with the finite last details. It would not have been possible to put it all together without her.

I am not sure where my special fascination for Hawaii came from. I've never been there, though I feel a special peace about it. Maybe it is because the ocean fully encompasses the islands that make up Hawaii, and the ocean is one of the places where I feel God's presence. Regardless as to its origins, I used my passion for Hawaii as the central theme of the vow renewal celebration. I researched Hawaiian faith and faith rituals along with their meanings and uses. I also researched the islands and wove all the intricate details into a beautiful celebration.

Every detail I chose to incorporate held great significance to me. In fact, each one became a drop in my bucket of leaving the past behind and the bucket of hope for a better more solid future. The kind of future one attains with solid roots in the ground. Visualize the effort that I put into each of the intricate details. The amount of energy I spent on each one directly corresponded with the energy I was investing into starting my life again. It was hard work, but fun—and with many rewards.

This vow renewal was different from our first wedding in that during our first ceremony, there were entirely too many conflicts between family members. This led to several uncomfortable moments during our wedding reception in 1997. This time we wanted only those people who were optimistic and conflict-free to celebrate with us. There were two exceptions to our policy of no family in attendance. First was my dad, because he had contacted me about three months into my blindness. Once he learned of my situation, he maintained regular contact with me and did what he could to help from Indiana. Second were Sherry's parents, John and Nancy, because they have a marriage that Chip and I aspire to emulate.

Our bottom line for attendance was this: we only wanted people who had been actively involved in our healing process. They surrounded and loved us throughout those difficult days in a way I had not previously known was humanly possible. Our choice of guests was perfect, because not only were we celebrating our anniversary, but we were also celebrating the recovery of my lost physical abilities.

The vow renewal was beautiful with Hawaiian traditions. I ordered fresh flowers shipped in from Hawaii. We held the ceremony on the beach, under an arched huppa with sheer white fabric draped over the top and embellished with greenery and flowers. On either side of the huppa, three tiki torches were filled only with flowers. Under the huppa was a table with a large open shell that held one lei made of green tea leaves that we used in our lasso ceremony and two fresh flower leis.

Also on the table under the huppa were two small shells, each filled with different colored sand. Chip had blue sand, I had white sand, and the central jar had earth-color sand to represent Christ. We alternated pouring our sand into the jar to represent our connection through Christ.

Okay, so every planned event generally has a few minor glitches. Ours had quite a few, but I think they made the event a perfect representation of what we were celebrating. It was the culmination of a season with major life struggles, from which we were emerging into a beautiful new beginning on the other side. This was a celebration of brokenness transformed into wholeness, in both our marriage and my health.

We faced three major obstacles. The first was the ocean's tide. While we were setting up our altar and arranging guest seating, the tide was coming in—not going out. Yep, we had to reset everything higher on the beach before heading off to get dressed. The second was the lack of a sound system. Air current from the tide washed all sound out, preventing our guests from hearing the service. The last thing we failed to take into consideration was my physical strength; even though I had gained freedom from full-time wheel chair use, I quickly tired. I had not regained enough strength to walk long distances in the sand.

Because we didn't have a sound system, our guests could not hear the announcement of our arrival when we blew the conch shell. In addition, it reduced the impact of sending our invitation to Father, Son, and Holy Spirit. Hawaiians do this by blowing into a conch shell three times. For us, it became thirty attempts by six different people, yet no one could make the horn loud enough. Our efforts seemed futile as we blew the shell in the direction of our guests, whose backs were facing us. I am not sure if they ever heard the shell horn, but it was priceless watching our very serious attempts, which made our cheeks puff out like a blowfish. We finally decided that either they had already heard it or it was not going to happen, and so we finally began walking across the sand to the huppa.

Chip and I started the ceremony by placing one of the flower leis on each other. We later sent these leis out to sea as an invitation to our deceased family and friends to join our celebration. For the lasso ceremony, Pastor Ron Wilson wrapped the lei in an infinity symbol around our wrists as he prayed a blessing over our re-union.

The ceremony concluded with a very special tradition: the wreath ceremony. My friend, Brenda, prepared a beautiful floral wreath with fresh flowers on the outside and a little biodegradable shelf in the middle. The middle section was to hold tissue paper, on which we wrote past hurts and trials. Under normal circumstances, the little papers were ignited in flames as the wreath was sent out to sea. It was not permissible for us to have fire on this beach, so, instead, Chip threw the wreath as far as he could into the surf.

This particular tradition was quite suited for us, as it was our opportunity to write down every trial, fear, and hurt that we had experienced in the prior year. Hawaiian tradition says that when the wreath returns to the shore, those past hurts will be gone, permanently lifted away. How awesome to couple a wedding anniversary with a celebration of new life! It marked a solid time we could celebrate every year as the new start for our lives together.

In the reception hall, we named our tables for each of the Hawaiian Islands, and provided fun facts about each. Our servers were dressed in Hawaiian clothing instead of dress suits, and our menu was planned as if we had just arrived for a Hawaiian luau on the beach. There were no worries, only happy times. In all, I could not have asked for a more perfect way to celebrate life's trials and victories. I felt so free and immensely blessed to do as much as I did. I consider that ceremony a liberation of sorts from the oppression I had felt over the prior months.

I stress the many intricate details invested in this celebration because it marked an end to one of the darkest periods in my life. It was as if every detail fulfilled in the execution of this celebration was one more drop in the bucket of healing for me, each one giving me more strength and more motivation to use my experiences to help others. From this celebration forward, the pendulum clearly shifted.

Over the next several months, the swelling in my nerves continued to diminish, allowing many of my abilities to return completely. With each one, I could feel my heart changing for the better. Looking back, I cannot believe the kind of a person I had become before the diagnosis. All of my past flaws were coming to the light. My heart cried out in apology to every person I had ever wronged or hurt. For those I could not personally contact, I prayed that the Lord would somehow let them feel my apology.

I started a personal journey, acknowledging and scrutinizing who I was becoming. Although this part of the journey could last indefinitely, it was time to apply the life the lessons I had learned through the recent trials.

This is young two-and-a-half year-old me. In the house I called my castle.
(Left to right) Gretchen, Jon, my daddy.

This is four-and-a-half year-old me. I had already developed a strong opinion against my mother by this point.

These are pictures taken of me in the two years around when my parents were divorced. The time when I was so depressed that I tried to kill myself.

This photo was taken during a modeling photo shoot
my sophomore year in high school, 1988.

April 2, 1989 Tar Hollow Moravian church camp. Picture
on the left is Gretchen at host home. This reflected a
genuine happy smile, something that did not happen often
before this time. Picture on the right is the camp lodge.

These were my little cherubs who protected me in my blindness by making grunting sounds when anyone approached me. One sat on either side of me. Mai Tai is in the front and her mommy, Zoey, is behind her.

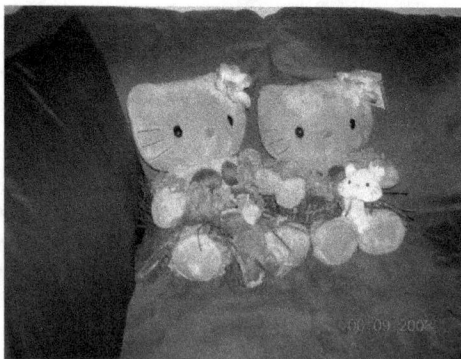

These are the Hello Kitty stuffed animals. Survivor is on the left with the dinosaur and Kelekena is on the right with a white kitty.

This is the surf board I painted when I had no depth perception and I could not see color. My daughter handed me the colors when I asked for them.

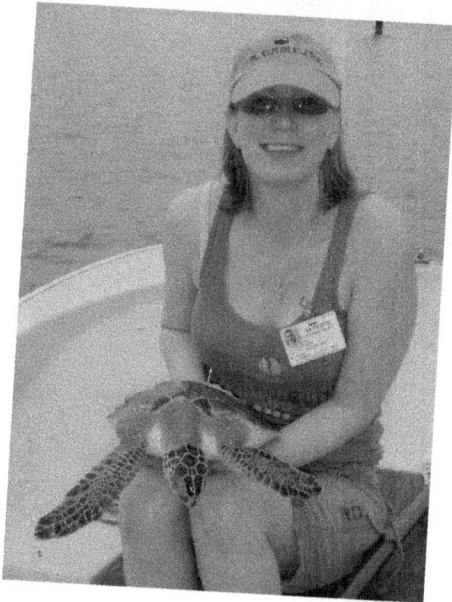

Me working with sea turtles in Spring 2010.

Spring 2005, releasing my lamprey larvae (babies) back into the field. Pictured left to right, Dr. Gordon Weddle,

I was injecting the fish larvae into the substrate, where they live for several years.

I walked my first 5K race in 2009, two and a half years after the major M.S. issues. I completed it in one hour and twenty minutes. I walked behind the wheel chair but never sat in it. (Left to Right) Gretchen, David.

Two years later, spring 2011, I completed the same race as above in 45 minutes. (Left to Right) Chip, Gretchen.

My first 8K race. Space Walk of Fame April 9, 2011. I completed it in 1:25:15. I'm so happy to have finished.

This picture was taken at Omega hospital on the day of my discharge, March 2008. (Left to right) Dr. Sullivan, Gretchen, Chip.

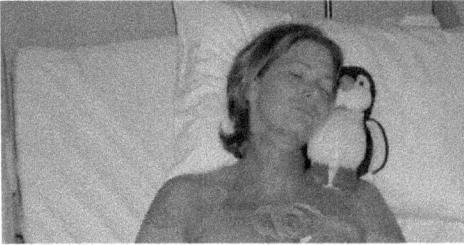

Coming out of surgery March 5, 2008.

This was taken in New Orleans after my first surgery, March 2008. It was the night before driving back to Titusville. (Left to Right) Mark, Jan, Chip, Gretchen.

Our wedding ceremony December 1997. Left to right Gretchen, Cristi, Gretchen, Rana.

Pre-ceremony picture for our vow renewal in 2007.

Pre-ceremony pictures. This was the most walking I did without my wheel chair since the medical crisis struck. Walking was slow times supported by Chip.

2007 ceremony at a glance on left. The right is the lasso ceremony.

Me wearing my peacock colors for graduation from graduate school, spring 2013.

Graduation, spring 2013. (From left to Right) Brett, Gretchen, Ryan.

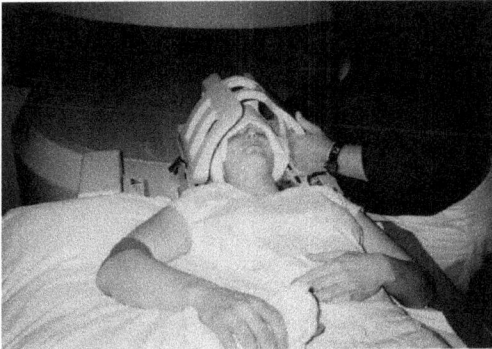

Me in the MRI, 2001. They were nice enough to let me take my ducky with me, seen in my right hand.

Me resting, during a study session, with my two little cherubs, Zoey and Lani, after a day at the infusion center, spring 2011.

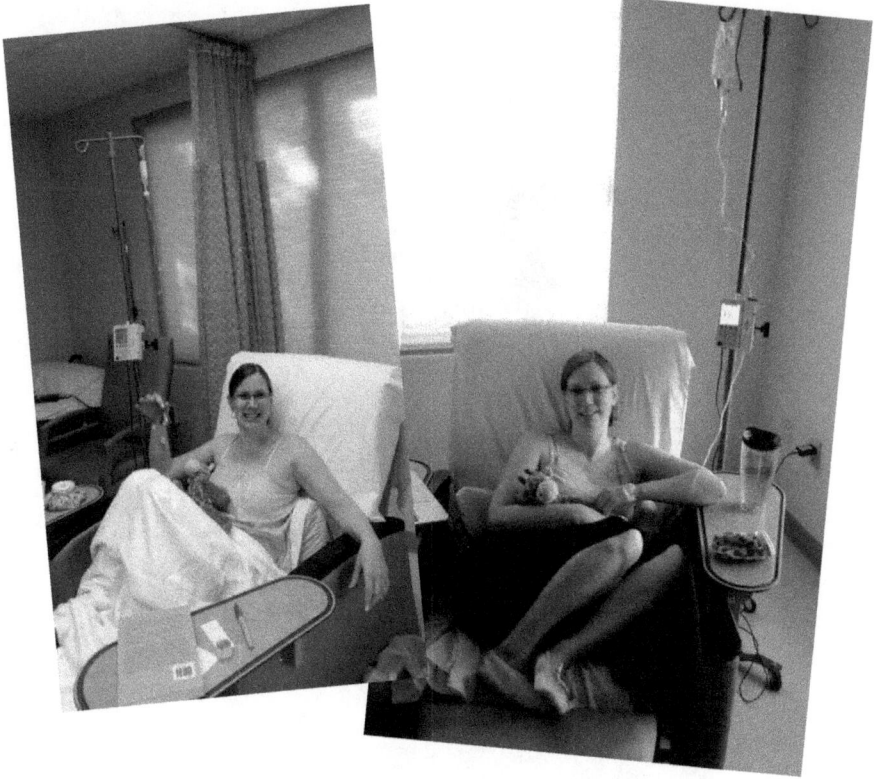

Above is my seat at the infusion center, September 2015.My nurse gave me a teeny tiny hand bell for when I needed something. That was the start to silliness for the week.

Above was taken on the last day for this round of steroids September 2015. Clearly, there are good days and not so good days. By this day, I was not feeling so good, that's a forced smile.

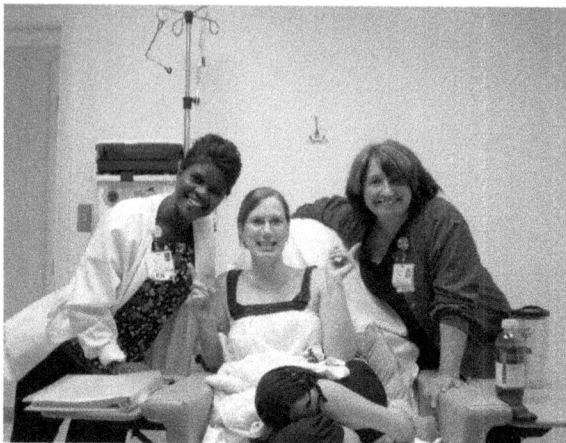

Me at the infusion center with my two nurses, summer 2014.
(Left to right) Sylvia, Gretchen, Jeanine.

Me at the infusion center spring 2015.
(Left to right) Jackie, Tammy, Gretchen.

Wanda was taking pictures of my family on the river, 2013. We got one with her too. (Left to right) Gretchen, Wanda.

This picture was taken at the celebration of life for my dad in August 2014. (Left to right) Rana, Cristi, Gretchen, Kachina.

Cristi and I with our daughters in August 2015.
(Left to right) Ashley, Gretchen, Cristi, and Sarah.

Me and Chip going to my very first concert ever, Spring
2015. We went to see Harry Connick Jr. at the Kings Center
in Melbourne, FL. What a Fantastic way to celebrate the
anniversary to our union and to my new life.

Chapter 12
Sharing My Story

In the fall of 2007, Pastor Jim, from Indian River City United Methodist Church in Titusville, was preaching a sermon series called "Facing the Giants." He called to ask if I was willing and able to offer my testimony. The concept of public speaking about a difficult time in my life was outside of my comfort zone. Regardless, I opted to say yes, because I believed that was what God wanted me to do. Pastor Jim paired my testimony with the talk on the giant of isolation, stating that he felt this giant was probably the largest of them all.

In his sermon, he discussed how we could face many things if we know others are with us and we are not alone. He went on to say that even strong people could find themselves in a place of isolation. This was leading up to the point of "power in partnership." Everyone needs someone to guide him or her *and* someone to lead. For the sake of the series, he called the partnership a huddle.

In my testimony, I explained that for months I was not only blind, but I was unable to do the things that people did every morning before going to work, school, or church. I shared that not only did I lose physical abilities, I also suffered from agonizing pain. I could not receive the comfort of touch without enduring excruciating pain. I also explained that I oftentimes found solace at the kneeling rail. I regularly went there to pray, "Lord, I am without words. Please search my heart for what I am trying to say." These were details from the start of my own huddle.

The church had four services on the weekends. When the time came for me to give my testimony, I remember asking myself if I was ready. The first service was difficult because the memory was still too fresh for me to maintain composure. The last service was difficult because I poured myself out in the prior three services. This experience completely drained me emotionally. No matter how difficult it felt to give the testimony, the fact that there were not many dry eyes through all four services was evidence that it clearly touched the congregation.

One man stood out the most. After the fourth service, he followed me to my vehicle, where he thanked me for my testimony. He said that his wife was currently going through something that he really did not understand. However, he believed that my testimony would better enable him to help her.

For several months following my testimony, I received further confirmation when total strangers approached me. Some announced that they came to my home to help when I was blind. Others had heard my testimony and thanked me because it helped them in some capacity or another. It felt good to know that my hardship was a blessing to others!

In October of 2007, two months after I gave testimony, a fantastic couple, Inez and Joe from Titusville, Florida, asked if they could sponsor Chip and me for a "Walk to Emmaus Weekend." We had met this couple at our church when they were among those helping our family. After our first meeting, they continued to check in on us regularly. There were times where we felt God specifically assigned them to care for our family and keep us lifted in prayer.

The Emmaus Weekend they sponsored us for was a three-and-a-half day journey with Christ. All participants, rather pilgrims, stayed at a retreat facility overnight Thursday to Sunday. The first night was intended for introductions and offering a chance to leave behind the monotony of daily life while preparing to open ourselves to an intimate connection with God. The first full day was for those on the journey to encounter God. The second day, we encountered Jesus. On the third day, we encountered the Holy Spirit, who would remain with us on our earthly walk.

To allow for the least amount of distractions, the meetings were not co-ed; they took place over two weekends, with the men attending the first weekend and the women on the second. After the life I had lived for the prior year, I was excited about going—until Chip left. It was the first time I had been alone since my blindness. I became angry and afraid and did not want to be home alone with my kids.

What made this weekend a bit more difficult was that I was awaiting results from a DNA blood test. This test was for the BRCA breast cancer gene[6], which runs in my mom's family. I had a feeling the results were in when I saw the mail carrier. When I opened the mailbox and saw the envelope from the DNA lab, I felt a proverbial carpet

---

[6] Breast cancer organization contact information is in Appendix B.

under my feet yanked away. This left me feeling as if I was aimlessly floating, with no solid structure to ground me.

Now that Chip was away for his Emmaus weekend, the lab results were in my hands. I knew in my gut what the results were going to reflect, but I did not want to see it. I put the envelope on the counter and walked out of the room then back in again. I stared at the envelope and tried to read through it, as if I had super powers. That is when I decided it was time to open the letter. As I read the results, I dropped to the floor and cried.

I had tested positive to the BRCA 2 gene, which is the gene responsible for both female and male breast cancers. I am sure I sobbed out of fear for my children's future as well as for the feeling of relief. I finally knew for sure. However, I now had another trial to face.

My relationship with my mother was already deeply broken. When I read the results, I felt that wound reopen. For a minute. Then I immediately gave it over to God because I knew I did not have the strength to handle my feelings. It was not fair and I had to forgive my mother or risk squelching my own healing from this new diagnosis by holding a grudge against her.

My second thought was for my kids. "What about their futures?" I asked myself. I have one boy and one girl but that did not matter with this gene because it affects both genders. Suddenly my mind rolled fast forward and I started blaming myself for what could happen to my children. The timing of this news was horrible because I still had two more days before Chip would return home. I needed his support.

The "poor me" frustration turned full throttle as those thoughts and concerns continued to recycle through my brain. Why did the results have to be positive? Why did I have to get these results while Chip was away? Yet, admittedly, I had strongly suspected the positive results. Suspecting and knowing were two different things, however. I had been hanging on to hope that I would evade that gene. Now I worried about my future. Why did I have to go through this after what I had been enduring for the past year and I was still not fully healed? But before I could verbally beat myself to death, Chip returned home.

I was able to sit down and talk to Chip about my fears that night. We debated whether this was the right timing for a preventative surgery. We speculated about how it would go and where the best place was to have the procedure. Did I have other options? We wondered. With a positive BRCA breast cancer gene and an aggressive family history of breast cancer, I had a decision to make. Soon.

Honestly, for me, the answer came easily. I believed the right decision was to proceed with the prophylactic breast surgery. This gave me control over my future in a positive way, even though it was a little scary. With the big decision out of the way, I could clear my mind enough to go enjoy my Emmaus weekend.

Once again, Chip was fantastic in the many ways he was supportive. All he wanted was for me to be comfortable with my decision and know that he could physically be there to support me. Once the decision was made, he helped me research locations, and he arranged for time off from work with his employer.

The Emmaus Weekend was supposed to be a good thing for me, especially after the news I had received the previous weekend. However, after I arrived at the camp, I quickly changed my mind. So many fears filled my head. I had only been taking MS medication for a few months and felt as if I was still too new to the process. Because the weekend was intended to be on God's time, the pilgrims, including me, were advised not to have watches or cell phones. I had to rely on the leaders to tell me when it was time to take my injection. How could I trust people I did not know? There were so many people, and I knew no one. Whom could I trust? Chip brought my wheel chair along with me for "just in case" while I hoped not, only because I did not want to give up control of that, too.

But God is good. He worked very fast in me. The first night He connected me with a woman named Karen Apodaca, my next silver lining. Now I am not sure what the connection was, other than I still believe she was an angel sent directly from Heaven. When I talked to her, I felt like I had known her for a lifetime already. It was easy and comfortable to talk to her. Before long, I was filling her in on all my heart's worries. She was so sweet, listening, and then offering calming and loving words. After my talk with her that first night, I started to relax a little.

The next day, I felt a victory for having completed a first night. In fact, I was actually starting to notice all the peaceful details of the location. The camp was on a lake with beautiful oak trees all around. In the middle of the lake was a cross that lit up at nighttime. There were no electronic devices, cell phones, or watches – much like God's time. It hit me that I had no appointments, no commitments to fulfill, no doctors to see, or blood to be drawn. I just needed to relax and enjoy this time while I was there.

On the evening of the second day, I stood up in front of all the ladies and gave my testimony. It was a brief description of my experiences during the past year, and then I revealed the news I had received the previous weekend. What better place to share that kind of news than around other ladies? Especially those who had already been on that life walk.

After my testimony, the leader ended our evening talks early because she said the depth of my testimony was something that influenced everyone in the room. The Holy Spirit was pouring into that space. Instead of continuing the talks, we spent time in communion. Several ladies approached me to say that they had been down the walk of a mastectomy and they were doing great. Other ladies thanked me for my testimony and explained what an inspiration I was to them.

I had been through so much pain, was getting ready to go through more trials, and yet somehow I was managing to continue living life. Wow, that spoke volumes, they told me. These women were such a blessing to me. Through the courage I gained this night, I wanted to start living my life again without the "poor me" fit. Even with all that I had going on, I had a wonderful life to live.

Sitting in this holy place caused my attitude to soften for the remainder of the weekend. At closing, I announced that while I knew the Lord had control over our physical situations, he revealed to me on the weekend that he also covers my emotions. Surprisingly, that is a concept I had never before associated with God.

The Emmaus Weekend was fantastic. It filled me with the Holy Spirit and charged me to go out and use my trials to inspire and positively influence others. However, my first step was to address the positive BRCA results.

Chapter 13

The Next Wave

In the days after my return from the Emmaus Weekend, I spent many hours in prayer before I decided the right doctor to perform the prophylactic double mastectomy. This procedure removes healthy tissue in an effort to stave off the development of cancer. My intention was to find a doctor who would not only do the double mastectomy, but also the reconstruction. I knew I was too young not to opt for reconstruction. However, I did not want implants because I thought there might be complications from MS that would cause my body to attack itself. I was hopeful that we would find someone who could use my own tissue.

To reduce complications, I wanted to have the surgery near my home. However, I quickly learned that having the procedure done locally did not reduce complications. In fact, it added a level of frustration I did not want to deal with. One of the doctors told me I was too skinny and suggested implants. Another said he could do the surgery, but would have to cut muscle and relocate it with the fat to provide a blood supply. I did not want to do that.

If the muscle was inadequate, it would probably not be strong enough to recover from the surgery. If the tissue was good, I did not want doctors to damage it by cutting and moving it. One surgeon even suggested prosthetics. I thought, "Hello! I'm thirty-four years old. What is that going to do to my self-esteem?" I did not want to consider any of those options. Either I was going to give up on the search, or I had to search farther from home. Giving up was not an option.

One of my dad's friends had recently gone through a double mastectomy and reconstruction. The procedure she had undergone was experimental, but had an exceptional success rate. I inquired about the doctors and conducted my own research.

My dad's friend had undergone surgery at The Center for Restorative Breast Surgery in New Orleans.[7] When I contacted *The Center*, they explained that the procedure would include the double mastectomy and reconstruction. For my body, they would use gluteal fat by moving tissue from my bum to my chest. The blood supply was going to come from arteries, not muscle. Because these details fulfilled my personal requirements for having the surgery, I scheduled surgery for March of 2008 at *The Center*.

By the end of 2007, my pending surgery was occupying my mind to the point of nearly rendering me functionless. I decided I should get a job to fill my time until I left for New Orleans. If all went well, I could come home to a job waiting for me. After filling out several applications, I received an offer as a hotel front-desk supervisor.

---

[7] The Center for Restorative Breast Surgery information is in Appendix B.

I have to back up in my story here. My mother-in-law, Ruth, was a restless person who found it difficult to stay in one place--which made it easy for her to follow her dreams of traveling. She had created a bucket list of those things she wanted to do before she died. She was out pursuing the line item on her bucket list for moving to Alaska, but decided to stay in Montana instead. Then, for some reason unknown to us, she decided to return to Florida in August of 2007. Since she sold her Florida home before she left, she came to live with my family and me.

Five months after she returned, she learned from her cardiologist that she was tired all the time because her defibrillator lead was not connected to her heart monitor. He needed to replace the device so that when her heartbeats slowed, the device would keep her heart going. He scheduled her for surgery during the last week of January 2008.

As her surgery date neared, understandably, the more nervous she became. I heard her up at night pacing the floor and fidgeting in the refrigerator. On those nights, I crawled out of bed, poured myself a drink, and sat with her. I knew where my nerves were, with my own surgery just under five weeks away. So, I could only imagine how nervous she was, being two days away from hers.

In those late hours, I believe we found peace by sharing our anxieties over our impending surgeries. She talked about her fear of the electrical lead that was dangling loose in her chest. She believed it could just zap her to her death at any minute. I talked about my fears dealing with the removal of such a deeply personal female area of my body. What would that do to my self-image? Because Ruth was Chip's mom, I opted not to discuss my concerns over what impact this would have on my husband's views of my body. Even though I did not talk to her about it, I was deeply concerned about the impact this surgery would have on our intimate life and, ultimately, on our marriage.

I loved my talks with Ruth; they were deep, honest, and full of emotion. Sometimes women desperately need to make that kind of connection.

Ruth made it to and successfully through her surgery. She was done and now I was on the surgical deck. As my nerves were twisting in knots late at night, Ruth returned the favor of getting out of bed to talk with me. We focused on the major differences between our situations. First of all, I had to go out of state for my surgery. Some of my greatest apprehensions involved going into surgery with a surgeon I had never met, leaving my children at home for two weeks, and not having any support people with us in New Orleans. Ruth helped me talk through necessary planning. On a fun note, she took the time to suggest some good restaurants to try in New Orleans because it was one of her favorite places to visit.

Many of my concerns were resolved before we left. My mother-in-law's job didn't allow her the privilege of availability to be sole caregiver for our kids during this time. So, my dad and his wife, Phyllis, flew in to take care of the kids for the two weeks we were away. We gained support during the surgery from our local Emmaus community, which contacted the Emmaus community in New Orleans.

Pastor Jim offered assistance by sharing contact information for a pastor in New Orleans to support us.

⁓

The day came for us to drive to New Orleans in March 2008. Stress of the surgery itself was minimal, primarily because I fully believed the Lord was in control. I still had apprehensions over what my doctor would be like and how badly I would hurt. The ride to New Orleans helped to distract me from my apprehensions. Instead, Chip and I took the drive as an opportunity to discuss how we could turn this trip into a vacation especially since we had never been there before. Of course, while we were there, we took time to visit a couple of the restaurants Ruth had suggested, in her honor.

When we arrived, the streets were still busy with Marti Gras traffic, talk, and activities. The traditional Mardi Gras colors—purple, green, and gold—were everywhere, and people were still exchanging beads. Our accommodations were in the restored eighteenth-century French Quarter at the Place D'Armes. Several buildings made up the construction of this hotel. Of the different buildings, the one we stayed in was once part of a children's home. According to the check-in clerk, that building was part of the haunted tour. She shared with us that hotel patrons in the past told her about a little boy who played with his ball up and down the hallway. I very much enjoyed hearing so many details of the area's rich history, but my looming pre-surgical activities were fighting for my conscious thought space. Thankfully, I was mentally able to soak in my surroundings.

First thing in the morning, *The Center* sent a limousine to transport Chip and me to Omega Hospital, where I met with my surgeon for the first time. I had knots in my stomach and felt vulnerable when the doctor asked me to disrobe. Of course, I was there for a double mastectomy and reconstruction from my tail end. How would he be able to do that without first seeing the parts?

Once I disrobed, Dr. Sullivan from *The Center* began drawing surgical lines on me as if I was the canvas for his masterpiece; in truth, I was exactly that. Though I felt uncomfortable about this part of the procedure, the doctor and his staff were fabulous at helping me to feel as comfortable as possible under the circumstances. In fact, I felt quite pampered. Like royalty.

After meeting with the reconstruction surgeon, I went upstairs to meet with the oncologist who was responsible for the double mastectomy. He talked to me about what it meant to test positive for the BRCA 2 breast cancer gene. Before this appointment, I did not know that the BRCA gene had a connection to ovarian cancer. With several occurrences of ovarian cancer in my family, I opted to have my ovaries removed. However, that procedure would not take place during this stage of surgery. After that meeting ended, we pre-registered for the next morning's surgery. And then the limousine returned us to the hotel.

Knots that developed earlier in the day had resurfaced making it difficult to eat. However, Chip and I still took time to walk around a few blocks just to see the area. While we walked through the town, it was fascinating to learn that they were filming a scary movie a couple blocks from where we were staying. When we returned to our hotel room, we prepared everything for the following morning, and then went to bed.

I could not sleep. Too many thoughts circled through my head. I thought about how awesome the doctor and facilities were and how wonderfully they had treated both Chip and me. Then I started worrying that I would sleep through my alarm clock. I certainly did not want to miss this surgery. Yes, I seriously thought that!

Just as I started to doze off, I heard people talking outside the window. I realized they were part of a ghost tour in process and listened in. The tour guide was just outside my window, telling the story of my building. If you were not familiar with this hotel, you would not know from the exterior that you were standing in front of a guest room. I decided it might be fun to start playing with the blinds and lights. One person noticed, and poked the person next to her, pointing at my window. For a few minutes, my antics got my mind off not being able to sleep. When the tourists left, I went back to bed and soon fell asleep.

The morning came early, and I was extremely tired. However, I was not worried about the lost sleep because I knew I would be asleep for several hours during surgery. The limousine picked me up at the hotel at 5:30 that morning, in order to get me to the hospital before 6:30.

Shortly after we arrived at the hospital, a pastor came into my room to pray with me. Pastor Jim had given us his contact information to connect with when we arrived in New Orleans. During this pre-surgery visit, he read Psalm 23 in a way that I had never heard before. It was almost as if I was hearing the Lord speaking to me, reassuring me that he was in control. It gave me a sense of peace and, oddly, an excitement to go under the knife.

Walking down the hallway to the pre-op room, I thought, this peculiarly felt like I was corralling myself for the slaughterhouse. That silly feeling did not last long, because the nurses and anesthetists immediately came in and began pre-surgical preparations by asking a series of questions, taking vital signs, and starting my IV. I had not processed that it was time when they started wheeling me down the hallway to the operating room.

One of my greatest concerns involving this surgery was the considerable amount of time that Chip would be by himself while I was under anesthesia. I wanted nothing more for him than to have someone to sit with him and help preoccupy his mind. He is not comfortable in crowds, so I hoped for smaller connections that were more intimate.

God answered my prayers by sending three men from a New Orleans Emmaus community to come sit with Chip. One of them, Mark Bugg, stayed for the entire nine-and-a-half-hour surgery, and was there to meet me when I woke up. Later that night, he returned with his wife, Jan, to meet me.

The amount of love this couple showered us with was nothing short of divine. Though I imagine after talking with someone for nine-and-a-half straight hours, you can no longer say you are strangers; you become more like family.

This couple exuded a selflessness I rarely see. They were in the middle of their honeymoon when they opted to come and be our support team. They lavished us, a couple they had just met, with agape love. We quickly developed a deep and intimate connection that no words can articulate; maybe divine beauty. I loved watching how Jesus chose to take care of us through this fabulous couple.

⌒‿‿‿⌒

Before going under anesthesia, I made a passionate request not to have narcotics; I do not like the control they take away from me. After that conversation, I said good night and whispered, "When you are in there and see God, tell him I said hi." After the lights went out for me, it felt like only minutes had passed before I opened my eyes again, though it was actually more than nine-and-a-half hours. Within minutes of coming off anesthesia, I woke up chattering incessantly with anyone who would listen—and some who would not. I think I even talked to my twin brother on the phone.

After waking up, my biggest complaint was dry mouth. The Sahara desert dryness led to jokes about how much alcohol the doctors had given me to induce that case of cottonmouth. When I talked, it felt as if I was spitting talcum powder. My tongue could not freely move, which prevented proper enunciation. I became moderately annoyed because it slurred my speech so badly that people could not understand me. Yes, I was a hot mess, but a happy one. Literally, every other word ended with a sip of water.

Once the procedure was complete, I had a checklist of activities to follow for proper healing to take place. The textbook version allotted a certain amount of time post-surgery for each milestone. Within four hours, I had surpassed the first day-and-a half of checkmarks. The list included such things as managing pain, being active, drinking enough, and emptying my bladder. After quickly attaining those milestones, the doctors removed both my catheter and IV, giving me liberty and freedom to move about the unit.

Chip was a trooper in how he woke up as much as I did. He reminded me of a mother who sleeps with one eye open. Every time I would move or whimper, he jumped to make sure he could give me what I needed. Every hour on the hour, he helped me unhook my leg pumps so I could walk a few laps around the hospital unit. The first time I took a stroll, I felt as if all of my insides were going to drop out of my rear end. However, it was difficult to keep focus on my rear end. For the first time in my life, I could not see my feet due to what felt like elephants glued to my chest. This was definitely an augmentation baby.

The entire situation was quite surreal: going to sleep with breasts and waking up with breasts that had multiplied in size. They were so large that I felt like they arrived at my destination about five minutes before I did. Ahh, the thrills of swelling.

Twenty-four hours after the surgery, walking became much easier for me, accompanied by only minimal discomfort. I honestly felt good and didn't need much more than a strong dose of Motrin for my pain; I attribute the regular walking to this successful progression of healing.

I saw my oncologist on the second night, during one of my walks. He looked at me and said, "I was told I had a patient who is wearing down my carpets. That must be you." He was not the only one who remarked about the frequency of my walking. I am a firm believer that exercise releases endorphins to help reduce pain and speeds the healing process.

To help post-surgical healing, my neurologist told me not to take my MS injections for two weeks before the surgery and two weeks afterwards. I admit a level of concern crossed my mind about how my body would respond to the trauma of surgery. I was pleasantly surprised to see that my only neurologic symptom was tingling in my skin. That symptom quickly diminished when I got up to walk.

Care at the hospital was superb. The staff offered exceptional treatment and services, both to Chip and me. They always greeted us with a smile and sincere concern for how I was feeling—and Chip, too, for that matter. The room was like a high-class hotel, complete with a Murphy bed for Chip, a television, a microwave, and refrigerator. We both ate exceptional food; all meals were prepared off the hospital grounds and catered in. To date I can say this was one of the best experiences in my life, something that most people cannot comprehend when talking about such a long and potentially traumatic surgery.

We remained in New Orleans for ten days, including our arrival a day early, to enjoy the festivities of Mardi Gras on the streets. The second day was full of pre-operative visits. Day three covered the surgery. Then seven days of recovery followed.

Before my discharge, my doctor removed the drains from under my breasts. However, when I went home, I still had the two drains in my hips. On the drive home, I kept telling Chip I felt like I was a birdie on a wire. That was because the drains went through the sides of my hips and ran parallel with the incisions under the skin in my bum. In this way, when I was in the seated position, it felt like I was sitting on skinny tubes.

The Center spoiled me by carting me around town in limousines, with a chauffeur who opened all the doors while helping me in and out with such sensitivity. Chip and I were able to experience New Orleans for the first time, and gained a new lifelong friendship (family-ship) with a super-fantabulous couple. No doubt, this couple was a silver lining for both Chip and me.

When I am asked if I would do it again, I say, "Yes, without a doubt—as long as it is at Omega Hospital with the team of doctors and staff from *The Center*. They were collectively significant silver linings for both Chip and me. The gray cloud that had hung over my head for ten years, dangling the threat of breast cancer, was now gone.

Chapter 14
Bonding Through Bandages

Ruth had her first surgery in mid-February of 2008. Chip and I left for New Orleans the first week in March just after Ruth had started to develop an infection at her surgical site. The antibiotics her doctor prescribed were unsuccessful in preventing a deeper infection. He scheduled her for a second surgery, to remove the entire defibrillator device.

Two weeks after I returned from my surgery, Ruth and I resumed our late-night talks to help her with her nerves. It is amazing the number of topics that can come up when you are scared about something. I cannot help but think God was in the driver's seat during those conversations, making it possible for us to laugh through our tensions.

Ruth came home from the hospital with an open wound because the doctor wanted it to heal from the inside out. He said this would help reduce the risk of redeveloping infection. Initially, a home-health nurse came out to change her dressings, the goal was for me to take over that role. The nurse directed me in how to apply the wet/dry dressing change. She said, I needed to do this three times a day. She would return every other day to check on the progress.

My time as a nurse in the 1990's, coupled with all my premedical coursework from the early 2000's, offered me in-depth experience with this type of wound care. This significantly helped Ruth's wound heal much faster than her doctor and nurse had anticipated.

Call it shared fears or bonding time, either way, our individual circumstances made my mother-in-law and I the optimum cohorts for planning individual responses to our surgeries. We were both in the active healing process simultaneously. I still had my hip drains, and she had a deep open hole in her chest. In our time together, during wound care, we shared our worries and vulnerabilities in a safe zone, knowing it was judgment-free. We talked about our goals for the future and the things that made us happy, sad, and hopeful. We shared fears over our surgical experiences and the hopes we had for the outcomes.

Changing Ruth's dressing became an art of dance. At first she looked away, so she did not see the hole in her chest—which had become a source of nightmares for her. In the nightmares, she could see her heart beating from the open hole. I was not afraid of hurting her because the area was still numb, a side effect from surgery. The issue was the number of times I inadvertently caught my own post-surgical hip drains on objects, which caused me sharp pain.

When Ruth realized I was hurting myself, our picture changed to a picture of selfless love. She held my drains, allowing me to place all of my attention on her wound care. Additionally, through her act of love, she redirected her attention from the hole in her chest to my drains. We had a crazy kind of symbiotic relationship that led to her doctor expressing amazement over how quickly she had fully healed. I believe it was because of God's love and special touch.

The worst part about Ruth's situation was that without the defibrillator in her chest, she had to wear an external device. She despised it and called it her "annoying baby." The silly contraption had a habit of making a loud siren noise when it was not correctly in place, usually while she was sleeping or in the shower. I prayed often for a resolve because I did not think she deserved the hell she was experiencing.

As her chest incision was closing, but before Ruth removed my hip drains, it was time to go "paint the town." Ruth and I shared a deep affinity for the same band, the Beach Boys. We heard they were coming to the Cocoa Beach pier and no medical situation was going to keep us away. Unfortunately, we did not fully think out how far we had to walk after parking.

We must have been a pathetic sight to watch as we waddled down the beach very slowly, with what felt like rubber legs. Half the time she was holding me up, and the other half of the time, I was holding her up. We were giggling like schoolgirls as we stumbled and swayed across the sand. Ruth was adorned with her external contraption and my drains looked like clappers protruding from my hips.

We made it to the concert, but did not have tickets, so we sat outside the fence with other people in our same position – no ticket. Our outing was truly an accomplishment. We sat, talked, and listened to a few songs. Then we decided that we had caught our breath, and though we would love to stay, we were really worn out and should probably go home. There are no words to describe how fortunate I was to experience this as my first-ever mother-daughter getaway. I felt like God was working to fill the void left by my mother's absence in my life.

—⁓—

Two-and-a-half months after the first surgery, I was contemplating round two of my mastectomy, the reconstruction phase. This stage greatly overwhelmed me. I had just celebrated my thirty-fifth birthday. This surgery would include a complete hysterectomy, to remove ovaries, fallopian tubes, uterus, and cervix. I was desperate for a mommy to reassure me, and went to Ruth. I spent countless hours talking to her. Never-ending circles of questions arose about a subject that was awkward to discuss.

I wondered whether the lack of hormone-producing glands would make me grow facial hair and develop a deep voice. Would I still be attractive to my husband? How would the surgery affect our intimacy? I felt as if I was about to become an "it" at the age of thirty-five and that thought made me anxious. Ruthie continually reassured me that everything was going to be okay. In fact, she predicted that things would be much better after this surgery—and, to a great extent, she was right. The much better part she was referring to was that I would no longer have the annoyance of a monthly female cycle. She also predicted that my massive mood swings would disappear. Fortunately, none of my fears became a reality.

The beginning of June rolled around all too fast. Before I knew it, Chip and I were packing and on our way to New Orleans for round two: the hysterectomy and stage two of breast reconstruction.

Chapter 15
Round Two in NOLA

To gain more experience in New Orleans, we made reservations at a different hotel. However, my gut did not feel settled. I am not sure if it was claustrophobia due to the low ceilings of the old hotel or something else. Regardless, I was too uncomfortable to stay there. Chip took me to another hotel, where more issues of the same kind arose—coupled this time with much more noise. I was already anxious about the pending surgery and just wanted calmness. Fortunately, as we stood at the check-in counter, we received a phone call from Mark and Jan Bugg, the couple who interrupted their honeymoon to help us during my first surgery in March

The New Orleans Emmaus community was the conduit for our connection with the Bugg's. They are middle-aged grandparents who, in my estimation, rank right up with the living angels that surrounded me during my blind invalid stage. Rarely do we cross paths with people who are as genuinely selfless as these individuals were. They offered a divinity so deep that there are no words to describe it. When Mark and Jan heard about our issues at the hotel, they graciously opened their home to us. We gratefully accepted.

This trip to New Orleans had a mental gray overcast from the start. Many aspects about it were different. First, we had problems with two different hotels before settling in at our friend's home. Then we learned that we could not register for surgery at Omega Hospital because of my insurance. Instead, I had to register at a public hospital. I found myself becoming more negative and nervous about this experience.

My pre-surgery appointment at *The Center* was the lift-me-up I needed. The staff always seemed to know the right thing to say. The doctors, nurses, and administrators were fabulous and sensitive to how their patients were feeling. They continued treating me like royalty and doing what they could to ensure my comfort during all of the pre-surgical appointments.

On the day of surgery, I arrived at the hospital early, expecting the procedure to be much shorter than the first one. This time we did not request a pastoral visit. Mark Bugg was the only person at the hospital with us before I went under anesthesia. He was a silver lining for Chip as he stayed through the entire surgery. Although we expected the procedures to take about four-and-a-half hours, complications occurred during the hysterectomy.

About the fifth hour into the surgery, thirty minutes after I should have been done, a hospital chaplain walked in to the waiting area. He sat at a desk and made a call, enquiring which family he needed to talk to about a patient who just died during surgery. Chip told me that when he heard those words he thought his heart had stopped beating and dropped to the floor. He thought that was the reason why no one had been out to talk to him about my surgery. When the chaplain walked into another waiting room, to talk to the family there, Chip realized he was actually breathing. After composing himself, he and Mark bowed heads and prayed for the family who had just lost their member.

Several years later, when we told my dad about this incident, he chuckled in amusement. As a former hospital chaplain, my dad knew it was the responsibility of the doctor to inform families of a death. Then the chaplain goes in to help the family with the next steps.

***

After about eight and a half hours of surgery, I was moved to the recovery room. Coming out of this surgery was more difficult than the first. When I woke up, I heard someone say, "Don't roll over. You just had surgery." That brought me into the present, where I realized I was not only in pain, but the pain was so intense it felt as if I had been mauled by a circus of animals. In my half-conscious state, I asked the nurse for pain medication. As soon as she injected it into the IV, I felt instant euphoria, followed by, "Lights out, man." I was knocked out cold.

It seemed like only a moment later that my head popped up and I asked for more medicine. The third time I awoke was different. I still had pain, but I did not ask for more medication. This was good timing, because my regular hospital room was ready and my nurse was jokingly getting stingy with the painkillers, saying that she would not let me have any more. That was okay. I honestly did not feel bad enough to take more. I simply enjoyed giving her a hard time about refusing to give a patient pain medicine.

In my room, I tried sitting up for the first time. BIG mistake! Something about when I sat up, I must have triggered my sneeze button. I didn't think I had any innards left because I was certain the pressure of my sneezing must have forced them out to where they were covering the walls, floor, and ceiling. Maybe I should have just stayed lying down because there was not a part of my torso that didn't feel full of holes.

But the situation worsened. A nurse told me I needed to start coughing. She handed me a pillow to support my abdomen and reduce the pain while I coughed. She was funny. Of course, I told her "NO." Besides, I didn't think I had anything left inside to cough out after that sneeze. She giggled and explained that it was for my own good, to keep my lungs clear, which would assist with healing.

Half-dazed by heavy coughing into the pillow, something hit me with absolute certainty. I am not sure the timing was optimal, but that was the timing God chose. He was calling me to do a breast-cancer awareness conference when I returned home. I did not audibly hear this call. It came to me as a nagging feeling from deep within my core. The only way that feeling could have broken through the shattering post-operative pain was if God had put it there. Maybe He intended it as a temporary distraction to help take the focus off my discomfort. Regardless, I looked up as if staring at His face and I asked, "Are you serious?" Clearly, he had more faith in my abilities than I did. I doubted that I could either speak publicly or produce a full program capable of holding an audience's attention.

As quickly as the thought entered my mind, I put it on hold, because the surgeon who completed my hysterectomy came into my room. She shared surgical details that explained my immense pain and the extra time under anesthesia. Apparently, during the hysterectomy, she identified a case of endometriosis that took several hours to clean out.

My stay at this hospital was not as pleasant as my stay at Omega. I just wanted to leave and I did everything I needed to do to gain a speedy discharge. When I left the hospital the next day, we returned to our friends' home. From a recovery standpoint, that was the worst day. The pain was so intense on every side of my body. I was on my knees with my arms crossed on a chair in front of me. I placed my head on my arms as I wailed out to God for mercy. Chip contacted my surgeons at Omega, who called in a narcotic pain medication to the pharmacy. That night I took one pill, covered my abdomen with a prayer shawl, and fell asleep. The next day I felt much better and was able to get up and be more active, using only Motrin for pain.

On the seventh day post-op, we went to follow-up appointments at *The Center* and the gyn-oncological surgeon. After both gave us the okay, we started our twelve-hour trip back home. This drive was so horribly uncomfortable that when we stopped for lunch, I wanted to shop for a pillow to cushion my abdomen. While we were eating lunch, I saw a Build-A-Bear workshop out the window. Like a nagging child, I begged Chip to let me go in and make an animal instead of buying a pillow. And he said okay.

We had just walked out of Build-A-Bear workshop and were walking through the parking lot when our kids called. They said a package had arrived from UPS. I told them they could open it and tell me what was inside. Rana had sent me a Build-A-Bear animal. I thought she knew me well, but I did not realize how well until this gift. Believe it or not, she sent the exact same animal with the exact same outfit that I had just purchased for myself: Hello Kitty with the Hawaiian outfit. Funny, I am not much of a Hello Kitty person but I do love anything tropical. Kelekena was the name she gave the kitty she made because that is what my name is in Hawaiian. I named mine Survivor because that is how I felt.

⌒⌒⌒

At home, I began planning the breast-cancer awareness conference. I decided on a date in October, Breast Cancer Awareness Month. Next, I needed a location. My church was always busy with a plethora of activities, and one of its primary missions is mothers of preschoolers. Since this was the perfect age group for my conference audience, I decided this should be the venue. Then I sought permission and looked for speakers. I collected educational materials to hand out, and created a power point presentation. Lastly, to entice attendance for such a heavy topic on a weekend, when people could be out doing something else, I ran around town collecting door prizes, predominantly from spas.

The conference, scheduled in October, ran perfectly. Three speakers, including myself, spoke to thirty women over two hours, which included a question-and-answer session and time for the raffle drawings. The audience was the perfect size, not too large or too small.

We had more than enough literature to go around, and people had opportunities to have their questions answered. It was a good feeling at the end to hear comments like, "I didn't know that before now," and "Now I have information to chew on before making a decision about my procedure." I went into the event believing I would be happy if I reached just one person. Coming out of the event, I was grateful to have reached several.

Through this event, God showed me a need and my capabilities to fill that need. This was the first project where I put all of my efforts as a direct response to a call from God. It was a picture of my hardship turning into a blessing. Now I knew I had to devote more time to sharing my experiences and knowledge with other people. I asked God to use me. He did. And He would continue to do so.

PHOEBE A Walker

Chapter 16

An Angel Called Ruth

Two weeks after the breast cancer conference in October 2008, I found the quickest way to get a Kirby sales person out of your house: receive an alarming phone call.

My friend Wanda lives about six doors up the road from me. We both had a Kirby sales representative at our house on that particular day. Throughout their sales pitch, we were texting each other to see which one would finish first. The poor man at my house was right in the middle of a demonstration—he had just put carpet shampoo on a large area of carpet in my family room when the phone rang. Because it was an unknown number, I tossed the phone to TJ. He immediately passed it back to me, saying the person insisted on talking to me. I could not hear over the vacuum, so I walked into the kitchen to take the call.

I did not know the out-of-state area code on the caller ID and did not recognize the woman's voice on the phone. She said, "I'm not at home, I'm in North Carolina. Your mom is at my house, and she's dead."

My jaw dropped and I fell to the floor in shock while I tried to register what she had just said. In my confusion, I thought, "How can this be?" I did not understand who the woman was, but I knew Ruth was not in North Carolina. She was working as a CNA with home-health care. Was this woman calling the right phone number? After asking the woman on the phone several questions, I finally established that she was one of Ruth's patients. The patient was visiting with someone in North Carolina while my mother-in-law was here in Florida staying at the patient's house, dog sitting. Then I remembered that is where Ruth said she would be when she left our house.

Ruth's patient had a roommate who heard dogs barking persistently from the patient's room. When she walked back to investigate, she found Ruth lying face down on the bed. The roommate called 911. When the EMTs arrived, they pronounced Ruth "expired." Because Ruth had been living with us, ours was the only number the patient had to contact in an emergency. Chip and I scurried around our house to grab what we needed and left for the patient's house, where we would find Ruth's body and the detectives.

Since we were the first ones contacted, I grabbed the phone book and made calls while Chip drove us to where Ruth's body lay. I called her mom and one of her sisters, and then I called Chip's two younger brothers. It took several hours to contact Chip's sister, because she was out of the country.

Our daughter Ashley, who had just turned eleven-years-old, was at the fall school social with friends, where we knew she would remain for hours. We left our fourteen-year-old son at the house to help the Kirby sales representative clean up and get out. This same night, we were supposed to put a large Hawaiian salad together for TJ's Junior ROTC luau fundraiser. Unfortunately, for TJ, this was also something we had imposed on him. We had mountains of salad materials and dishes that he needed to give to the Junior ROTC parent who was coming to our house to pick them up.

A police investigator let us in to the room to see Ruth's body. We gave him positive identification. From her body position, it looked as though she had been sitting on the side of the bed going through papers when she died. She appeared to have fallen sideways with her hand over her heart. When I saw this, I fell to my knees next to Ruth and began to cry. I put my hand on her head and could feel her skin was still warm. I was afraid. I did not know where she was in her walk with God. All I knew was that I wanted to be able to see her again someday. I prayed for her and begged the Lord to forgive her and take her home in the event that she had not asked it for herself. From a medical standpoint, I remembered that the sense of hearing is supposed to be the last thing to go. With the hope that she could still hear me, I told her that I loved her so much and while I would miss her, it was okay to go home.

Chip was very upset about the loss of his mother, but he did not respond the same way I did, which was with endless tears. I did not want to leave the side of her lifeless body, but he felt very uncomfortable around it. He opted to walk in to see her and then right back out. All he wanted to do was see the body to make sure it was really her. As the oldest sibling, he turned his attention to the duties of executor of his mother's estate. He wanted to make sure her end-of-life affairs were in order and each sibling was taken care of.

When I sat next to her body, I reflected on our conversations and remembered that Ruth did know about Jesus and even talked to him at times. She always said the most important words in the Bible were the ones printed in red. Regardless, we were not certain if she ever asked God into her heart. I believe we received the answer at the conclusion of her memorial service on October 25, 2008. Because Ruth did not have her own church and we were so active in our church, we asked our junior pastor, Reverend Tony Bowick, to perform the service. As we were walking out from the service, members of the church told us they saw a rainbow appear just prior to us walking out. There were no rain clouds in the sky. I took that as confirmation that the Lord had taken Ruth home.

      This loss of my mother-in-law was very difficult for me, although I was grateful that she was no longer in physical pain. I had been a part of my husband's family for nearly thirteen years when Ruth died. I watched her emotional heart change for the better in the prior two years, and I felt fortunate to have had her living in our home for the last fourteen months of her life. Recently she had started having a thirst to reconnect with her family and redevelop relationships. Until this point, she always said she preferred relationships with animals to those with people.

      While she lived with us, we became accustomed to eating meals at the dinner table, walking together, playing board games and lottery scratch-offs, and watching movies. One of the movies we talked about in depth was *The Bucket List*. We discussed our bucket lists. Ruth never did made it to Alaska, but after making it to Montana, she decided she didn't want to go to Alaska anymore. The incomplete part of her bucket list included going to Spain to visit her daughter and moving to Greenland. However, she decided that she would miss her family too much to go to Greenland.

Most of us remember Ruthie as someone who did her laundry with her pockets full. One day, a pen from Ruth's laundry exploded and stained one of Ashley's dresses. Ruth felt horrible about it and wanted to make things right for Ashley. The three of us went shopping for a new dress. We enjoyed talking through dressing room walls as if no one else was there. Until this point, Ashley and I had not experienced this kind of generational connection with family.

Ruth and I bonded the most during 2008, during our two surgical procedures each. Her first one was in January and mine was in March. Her second surgery was in April and mine was in June. With both of us requiring six weeks of recovery after each surgery, you can see where we overlapped. We found the experiences much easier to go through having each other to share pain, stories, and medical gauze for dressings. We made a great team through these healing processes.

Ruth was more than a mother figure to me she was also a friend. I was thankful for the late-night talks we had, no matter who was doing the leaning and who was doing the listening. I enjoyed her funny antics and our fun time out on the town, whether alone or with my friends. I appreciated the feedback that she gave when I was working on projects and how instrumental she was as a grandmother. I remember all the stories she shared with the kids. I grew so used to her being there, that I really missed her when she was gone.

The kids fondly remember their grandmother. They say they are still amazed at how they could hear her sawing logs through two shut doors; her snoring was legendary in this house. Ashley said she was glad she finally figured out where her shampoo was going: Ruth was using it. Moreover, both TJ and Ashley still laugh as they remember how Ruth was immensely technology-challenged. She continually locked herself out of all her favorite shows by setting the parent controls to "G"-rated programs only.

Ruth made me think, laugh, cry, and want to love even more. To me, she will always be a wonderful, beautiful woman. I have a void without her that no one can fill—that is the place I will seek her through Christ. For certain, she was a significant silver lining in my life, particularly in her last months with us.

Chapter 17
Sisters

After I returned from surgery in June 2008, I quit my job. By October, I wished I still had that job, to redirect my attention from the loss of Ruth. I believe God knew my heart needed more distractions, so he sent me a new assignment. Just as I was completing all the technical work on Ruth's financials, Pastor Jim, from my church, approached me about planning our involvement in the Titusville City Christmas Parade. I agreed to join efforts with a man who supplied banners for volunteers to carry. My primary goals were to find a way to get my truck to blend in with the people who were walking, and to find people willing to walk with banners.

I sewed three large banners that read "Faith," "Hope," and "Love" to cover each side of my truck and the cab. Personally, I did not get much out of my involvement in planning and participating in the parade, but it was a good distraction.

I have a friend and neighbor named Wanda Faison. She and I met in the spring 1998, when she and her family moved into base housing in Jacksonville, two doors down from my house. She and I maintained our friendship through the many moves both of us made over the years. When Chip and I had our vow renewal service in the spring of 2007, I invited her to be a bridesmaid. She flew in from

Hawaii, and fell in love with my house. Then she learned that the model home was across the street and went to checked it out. Wanda was so impressed that she decided to have her house built six doors down the road from me. Before she flew back to Hawaii, she signed a contract for that lot and the construction. She and her family moved into that house in fall 2007.

Wanda and I attend different churches. At the time, hers was much smaller than mine was. Wanda was leading a Christmas youth program at her church in December 2007, the weekend after the town Christmas parade. She asked if she could borrow my three banners for a youth function. While my family sat watching the Christmas program, I felt like I was supposed to offer my banners to her church. Following the service, I approached Pastor Wright and offered them to him. He was so humbled that he accepted the offer and then asked if I would make him another set of banners.

Something in me felt convicted that he was going to request the fruits of the spirit series. I told him I would be happy to make them, but cautioned him on a potential delay because I was working on getting into graduate school. He responded, "This first. Then graduate school." The voice did not sound like his. It sounded as if the Lord was speaking through Pastor Wright.

When I enquired which series he would like, it was – of course, the fruits of the spirit. Now I was certain God had just given me my next assignment. My heart wanted to do the absolute best I could to make these banners, as if I were making them for Him. Once they were completed, I took them to my church to have blessings prayed over them. Then I formally presented them to Pastor Wright's church. I felt blessed to be able to offer my time and this gift to them.

After completing the banners, I returned my focus to studying for the Graduate Record Exam (GRE). My desire to return to college goes back to when I moved in with my dad and realized how much I enjoyed learning. That was when I decided I would never stop working on continuing education. Flash forward to present day, and education became an excellent distraction to this disease that I live with. When I succeeded in class, it helped me forget the things the disease made difficult for me to accomplish. I saw how perfectly God knitted the breast cancer awareness conference, coordination of my involvement in the Christmas parade, and creation of the banners in the midst of a year of trials. Each activity perfectly matched timing with my abilities. They were beautifully orchestrated tools from God.

When I started working for the hotel at the end of 2007 and into 2008, I met a woman named Robin Rich. She was a night auditor who put in her two weeks' notice during my first week on the job because she was recently engaged and moving out of state. Robin and I shared only a professional relationship; I knew she was a good worker. On a personal level, however, she used to mock my faith. That did not bother me too much because I knew she only had a few more days working for me.

Almost two years later, in the fall of 2009, Chip and I joined a discipleship class at our church, where I was uncomfortably surprised to see Robin – who had been assigned to our small group. She had not married, and felt called to return. In spite of all the grief she had given me about my faith, she had a strong thirst to reconnect with God.

In our group, she was the one who flourished the most. Just like a sponge, she absorbed every detail of our lessons and scripture. She asked many questions and took detailed notes that filled every available white space in her discipleship book—including spaces between lines. When looking in her book, it was difficult to determine whether the published words outnumbered those she wrote by hand.

As our class progressed, I felt God's call for me to sponsor her for a Walk to Emmaus Weekend. I seriously questioned this feeling, and did not think my praying skills were fully equipped. In such, I used logic in the place of prayer to decide. Robin had an immense desire to learn more than it appeared our discipleship class could offer her. That impressed me enough to sponsor her for Emmaus in November 2009.

As a rule, those who work on an Emmaus weekend cannot also sponsor someone for that weekend. In this way, the individual (pilgrim) will have the sponsor's undivided attention during that time. I was working the November walk, but I believed that it was also my call to sponsor Robin. I received special permission to both sponsor Robin and work the weekend on one condition. I had to find a co-sponsor.

I searched for and found someone willing to co-sponsor Robin with me. It was Joy Lesky. This fantastic woman was part of a clown ministry that brought joy to those who were down, to those who were celebrating, and everyone in between. In fact, she was one of the first people to sit with me during administration of my IV medication at the infusion center. I always felt like a queen when she offered foods that would help calm my stomach from the medicine. She also massaged my feet to help me relax while I received the IV. I was overjoyed that she was willing to team up with me again, this time to co-sponsor Robin.

Robin suffered a great deal from spinal stenosis, a condition where vertebras constrict the spinal cord, creating intense pain most of the time. Regardless of the pain, she attended the weekend and did the best she could to remain as active as possible. In fact, while she was there, she participated by writing many poems and songs. It was fascinating how she could sit down and pour them out in less than five minutes without making changes during the writing process. The following are two of my favorites:

BRANCHES OF GOD'S TREE

We are branches of a large unimaginable tree
We bear fruit in many colors for all to see.

Our roots grow strong where they belong,
Beneath that heavenly trunk.
We delight in nourishing others
With all the nectar they have drunk.

We are branches of a large unimaginable tree.
We bear fruit in many colors for all to see.

It is so sad when a branch is bad.
It withers and rots on the ground.

183

We shake our leaves and pray for them,
But they are lost, never to be found.

We are branches of a large unimaginable tree.
We bear fruit in many colors for all to see.

It's a sign to us to see other leaves rust
As they bear fruit no more.
But we check our roots in God's pursuits,
And make sure they remain secure.

We are all branches of a large unimaginable tree.
We bear fruit in many colors for all to see.

We all have the chance when we see a glance
From a lost and needy soul
To fill their cups with love and trust,
For that is our eternal goal.

We are all branches of a large unimaginable tree.
We bear fruit in many colors for all to see.

ARMS OPEN WIDE

I'm standing here, arms open wide,
Letting Jesus deep inside.
We will both walk side by side,
Enjoying life's roller coaster ride.

Up and down,

Round and round.

No matter how far we go,

I am safe because I know,

High and low,

Fast and slow,

I'm facing life full speed ahead.

There is nothing that I dread,

Quiet and loud,

Humble not proud.

I'm facing life full circle now.

Thanks to God who taught me how

To stand here, arms open wide,

And let Jesus deep inside.

We will both walk side by side.

Now life's a smooth roller coaster ride.

On this same weekend in November of 2009, I met another very dear friend of mine, who oftentimes acts as a stand-in mommy. Her name is Jackie Haines. She is not as tall as I am and petite in stature. This woman has a metabolism on steroids for how much energy she has. Her personality is always full of excitement for Christ and abundant love of neighbor. It was on this weekend that I learned her husband had gone to be with the Lord almost exactly two weeks after Ruth died, in 2008. The only explanation for how quickly and deeply we all three connected, was that the Lord conducted it. The weekend deeply impressed Jackie by her renewed bond with Christ. The connection was so profound that before she left the camp, she signed up to work the next Emmaus weekend, in the spring of 2010. After returning home, Jackie, Robin, and I started regular weekly accountability meetings that drew us even closer.

At our weekly meeting, we talked about the times when we felt closest to Christ, when we felt farthest from Christ, what we were doing to stay connected with Christ, and what we could do in the week to come to build our relationship with Christ. We continually strove to become more like Christ, especially through our daily trials. Our accountability meeting was a safe place to confront and be confronted about areas that were not so Christ-like in our lives. Our tremendous growth could only have come from God.

The culmination of our meetings created the platform for the next stage of my life. My accountability group was a permanent silver lining that walked me through a significant transitional stage in my life. Through our continued meetings, I gained the strength and encouragement to dive in with absolute abandon of self while fully trusting God.

Chapter 18

The Call

For as long as I can remember, I have wanted to become a doctor. In fact, after I completed my associate of arts degree in Nebraska the summer of 2001, I was accepted at the University of North Carolina at Chapel Hill for the pre-medical program. When my neurologic issues began developing that fall, I decided to decline my acceptance. It was a very difficult decision, to turn down the opportunity to go to medical school. I felt defeated. The survivor in me said that even though I was not going to pursue my first dream, I could stay in the discipline and still make a difference in the field of biology. I went on to complete my undergraduate studies in 2005, with a Bachelor of Science degree in biology and a minor in environmental science.

Once we settled into our forever home in Titusville and my health became stabilized, in 2008, I started researching universities and programs. That is when I identified a conservation biology doctoral program at the University of Central Florida (UCF). The UCF biology department offered a sea turtle program that fascinated me. I worked diligently to get into that department. After attempts in 2009, I was finally able to meet with the sea turtle advisor about joining the team.

During the visit, I felt compelled to discuss my medical condition. I explained how one of my worst enemies was too much direct heat, but that I had assistive devices to keep me cool. From the beginning, I was open and honest about my disability and my plan to keep it controlled.

To make sure I was physically capable of doing the work, I met with the sea turtle team on several occasions. It was as if the sky opened and doused me with blessings every time they let me accompany them in the boats to collect data. I remember thinking to myself, "This is what it must feel like to be the recipient of Make-a-Wish Foundation." The blessing was so grand; I know I was beaming every day that I went out on the boats to survey the turtles. Each time I returned home with the sensation that my legs were still wobbling from standing in the boat for so long. Even so, I jumped up, punched the air, and shouted, "WAHOOOOOOOOOOOOOOOOOOIE! This was the best day yet!"

I do not deny the physical strain of the work, having to keep balanced while lifting the turtles onto the boat, taking measurements, and tagging them, sometimes in turbulent waters. However, this physical requirement can be difficult for anyone with or without a disease. If I could have made a full-time job of working part-time hours with the sea turtles, it would have been the perfect job. Bottom line, I cannot thank "Doc", Dr. Llewellyn Ehrhart, enough for giving me this "opportunity of a lifetime." After each day I was in the field, I gave thanks to God with tears of joy on my way home because this was not possible without God's provision of this silver lining.

In March of 2010, Jackie, Robin, and I went back to work a Walk to Emmaus Weekend. This time, I sponsored Wanda. This weekend was unique in a way that I cannot fully articulate. On a very special evening, I went to the kneeling rail to pray. I was the sole person there, but did not mind because I wanted some alone time before the rail filled up. God must have sent a message to the pastor, because he walked up to me and asked if he could anoint me. When I agreed, he began praying. This man prayed things no one there knew about me. He prayed healing from the broken relationship with my mother, he prayed about my specific educational goals, and he prayed about my specific concerns at the time. There is no reason I should have been shocked, but I was. I attempted to wrap my mind around what happened. However, by the end of the weekend, even with no clear understanding, I had let my shock go.

What I saw when we arrived home recalled the kneeling rail encounter. When we pulled into the driveway, my house looked very different. It was dark and hazy—like a scary movie. I traced around windows, doors, and flowerbeds with my eyes. Nothing was different. When I went inside, the lights were dim, and the same phenomenon occurred. Now that was odd. I thought, how did the inside of my house get hazy?

My surroundings remained hazy as I unpacked. Before I knew it, for no reason, I was crying. Horrible thoughts circled in my head like, "You're too fat and ugly." "You're diseased." "How are you ever going to finish a degree?" "You're going to go back to school. You'll get half way through it and not be able to finish. That is taking your family's money and flushing it down the toilet." And, "You are not good enough to do anything." That night, I cried myself to sleep.

No one in my family approached me during this time. In fact, it was so confusing to me; I could never articulate the details to them. I just needed to trust that God was in the middle of it somewhere and He would guide me to the right people to talk about it. Unfortunately, He did not immediately reveal those people to me.

When I awoke the next morning, I could clearly see around the house, but my head still felt foggy. Then I heard myself say, "I am going to seminary." The words shocked me, and I wondered where they came from. Was I not working with the sea turtles? Didn't it take me over a year to get the application in, and didn't I beat the odds by accomplishing what I already had? I had conflicting feelings, extreme joy at the prospect of seminary and immense loss for leaving the turtle program. That day, I applied for seminary, then immediately connected with several people who were familiar with seminary, to start enquiring about the process.

In the meantime, I bargained with God. Can I do both? Can I finish doing one more term with the turtles and then start seminary? Five weeks later, I received letters from both UCF and the seminary on the same day. Both were letters of acceptance. I cried hard for three days in my last-ditch effort to bargain with God to let me do both. However, I knew I couldn't truly give all of myself to either of them if I were doing both at the same time.

My heart spoke and while I was still uncertain. I figured the situation was a win either way. That afternoon, I called Doc and told him, "Like a woman in labor knows that her child is coming out, I know that I am going to seminary." I hope he understood. I love the sea turtles and the experience I had with them. In the future, I will accept any opportunity to work with them again. However, at the time when I was deciding which path to take, I knew my heart first belonged to God and I had to listen to His will for me. Maybe someday He will open up a way for me to work with turtles again. As of today, sadly, that opportunity has not come available.

Do you remember that little voice that filled my head with horrible thoughts after my Emmaus weekend? Well, it loved to antagonize me throughout seminary. After I started seminary, my neurologist decided it would be good for me to receive the high-dose IV solumedrol (steroid) every eight weeks for a three-to-five day dose, depending on my need. This was to help prevent school stress from exacerbating my symptoms.

The IV medication worked well. It served the purpose of getting me through seminary, although it came with its own set of issues. Every time I went on the steroids, I experienced a plethora of side effects: cloudy mind, dizziness, temporary exacerbation of symptoms, sinus issues, and thrush in the mouth, among others too personal to write here. At times, I found it difficult to focus well or complete assignments in a timely manner.

Whenever I took the IV steroids, the side effects prevented my ability to drive safely. This meant I had to ask someone to take me to the infusion center to receive the medication. Then, if I had a class on that same day, someone also needed to drive me an hour each way to and from Orlando, and sit in class for several hours with me. I had to ask that person to commit an entire day to me alone. I felt as if I were an inconvenience and a burden to the people who had to drive me. In these moments, that little voice resurfaced and told me that I could not finish school and I was wasting money.

In times like this, I needed to search for affirmation from God. I knew I was making the right decisions because he continued to bless me with people who lifted my spirits.

The unexpected blessings from people became my most coveted silver linings. The first one of this kind came during my first term at seminary and correlated with my first round of IV steroids. Shane Shepherd was one of the first students I met at the middle school when my family moved to Lebanon, Indiana, in 1985. I had not talked to him since before I moved into my dad's house in 1988. Then out of nowhere, in 2011, he found me on Facebook and asked for my address. Within a week, he contacted me to say I should be expecting a package within a couple days. Wow! I had value. I already felt loved by my family and local friends, but this was over-the-top special because it was not expected. The gift was not elaborate, but it made me feel like a queen. It was a king cake from New Orleans used in celebration of Mardi Gras.

Sometimes people need to understand that the smallest gestures can bring forth a much greater response than the more elaborate ones. Shane and Sandra Shepherd from Lebanon, Indiana, have no idea how much inspiration and motivation they gave me to keep walking and to stay on the right path. Their gesture showed me that I was worth all the implied inconveniences the voice within my thoughts continued taunting. At the end of the term, as academics became more challenging, I ruminated on what my friends did for me, and that ignited my soul to reengage my efforts to the term's completion.

Each term gradually became more difficult. Course work was more demanding. Responsibilities at home increased when we invited two teenaged boys to come live with us. And my neurologic issues became more serious. I started feeling fatigued, I lacked cognitive ability, and I was exhausted. If I was going to complete the goal of obtaining my graduate degree, I needed to stay strong and keep my focus only on the positives. The friends who became silver linings brought nothing but positives, like Sandra and Shane. They made it possible for me to attain this goal.

Seminary taught me about myself. During my pre-seminary years, I had created a religious bubble, where I believed I was responsible for seeking people to convert. Seminary popped that bubble. Now I believe that God's intention is for us to go out and live the Bible. Of course, knowing scripture is important, for personal accountability and for when people are interested enough to ask faith-based questions, I will be prepared to answer.

In my World Religions course, I learned that every religious affiliation has at least one part of eternal life right, but none has it all correct. I believe that in the end, all the different religious beliefs will meld together in some fashion. My class visited Buddhist communities and a Muslim mosque. It was a privilege to visit with other faith-based groups, to learn how they worship. Of my time at the seminary, I benefitted the most from this course. It was the one responsible for opening my eyes and popping my holy bubble.

Another course I gleaned much from was Cultural Studies, probably for very similar reasons as the World Religions course. Humanity differs in customs, habits, and ways of living, all around the globe. We might worship differently, yet we have a connection through love. I believe this is God's intention for us all.

During my final term in seminary, spring of 2013, I had to find a mentor and that mentor had to appoint a ministry advisory group for me. As a Methodist, I was seeking someone from the same denomination. However, I felt called to an Episcopal church and could not do both because it would prevent me from experiencing this course to its fullest.

After much deliberation, I met with Father Rob Goodridge, the Rector for St. Gabriel's Episcopal Church in Titusville, Florida.[8] He agreed to become my mentor for the term and assigned four ladies to be part of my mentorship team. Pat, Jo, Carla, and Marie, plus Father Rob collectively served as a tool that helped me prune my soul to be more in alignment with Christ. During our meetings, I was given assignments to work on and then discuss what I could do to put myself down and allow God to move in those situations. I didn't realize how strong my control issue had become. When situations came up around me, I wanted to resolve them but the reality is that God does not call us to do all things.

---

[8] Contact information for this church is in Appendix B.

Sometimes the call was not mine to answer—even though I was at a point where I wanted to fix or help everyone.

I learned much from Father Rob about how to stop "doing" and start "being." He also stressed my need to slow down and listen for God. One of the greatest lessons I learned was that I did not need to know the "why" of situations. In fact, he told me that I just needed to show up and be willing to let God do the work. There was no need to figure out how or why I would do something. If I showed up and God wanted to use me, He would guide me in the next steps.

If I did not show up, or was unwilling to move out of the way for God, then He would go around me and get the task accomplished using someone else. Ultimately, it is far easier to do our tasks the way God intended, through obedience to His call. I just need to show up, quit trying to do it for Him, and let Him do his thing.

Funny how simple that concept is, but it took me an entire term to get it, and now, I cannot seem to lose it! I am truly a new person from this experience. I imagine that was God's intention when He guided me to seminary in the first place.

Right now, I have no clear direction to follow after my studies at the seminary—or my studies in biology, for that matter. I imagine, then, that a concise occupational call is most likely a moot point for me, at least for right now.

The bottom line is that my ideal call is God's call. For the time, I still feel my purpose is to lift others in times of their own trials.

PHOEBE A Walker

Chapter 19

An Angel Called Karen

Going back to the fall of 2009, when I was spending hours studying for the GRE, I remember times when I felt my brain suffered from overload and needed some downtime. One of my favorite things to de-stress was browsing in consignment stores. We have several in the old downtown part of Titusville. One of them I passed by several times a month: a cute little house that the owner modified into a shop. One afternoon I felt a very strong urge to stop. This feeling was quite similar to the one that guided me to the Methodist church at the right time in 2006.

I decided not to ignore the feeling, so I went into the shop, which was packed to the gills with sophisticated yet fun articles of clothing and accessories. The owner must have been a shopper after my own heart, because I loved everything. If I could, I would have purchased everything.

During the second visit, I had the pleasure of meeting Karen, the owner. We got to talking about my plans of returning to school and how, for a time, I did not think I would be able to do anything again, let alone go back to school. By my third visit to the store, it became evident that my stopping by was no accident. Rather, God must have orchestrated it. Karen started asking me questions about my MS, more specifically, about my early symptoms. She was experiencing neurologic symptoms and was in the "we don't know what it is" phase—my most despised stage.

After I learned of her medical situation, my heart melted for her. I was still in the final stages of healing from my own medical crisis and fears left over from the worst days still resonated deeply within me. I wanted to do what I could to help her find a peace. I hoped she would not have the same depth of devastation that I experienced. But I did not know how to help her. Really, when I was going through my struggles, the best help came from those willing to sit with me without trying to make sense of my situation. I decided I could do that for her by just stopping into her store on a regular basis, almost daily. When I visited, I did my best to listen to her concerns and fears. Then I prayed with her.

A couple months down the road, I noticed she spent fewer days at the shop. This is when I had to listen for God's guidance on when to stop by. Usually this was in the form of a special tug on my heart that said, "Go to the store now, Karen will be there." That feeling was spot-on for accurately coordinating my visits. Every opportunity I had, I explained how I managed to live with neurologic symptoms as they appeared. In fact, no matter who asked me, my answer was—and is— always, "God!" I immediately followed that with positive mind-set, diet, sleep, chiropractic treatments, acupuncture, and exercise.[9]

---

[9] My chiropractor and acupuncturist information is in Appendix B.

One day, Karen invited me to her house. When I arrived, I noticed that she was walking the same way I did just before the worst of my symptoms hit in 2006. When she walked, one of her legs took a heavy step, and then she used her hip to lift the other leg and swing it forward. Meanwhile, her arms were overcompensating as she threw her bad leg forward, making her look like she was swimming. When I saw her walking this way, my heart sank to my stomach as I fully remembered what I felt like during my time with that symptom. It was annoying, to say the least. Unlike me, her walking never got better. It just continued to get worse. This is about the time when Karen told me they diagnosed her with Lou Gehrig's disease (ALS).

In our talks at the shop, I knew that Karen was not going to a church anywhere. Because her health was rapidly deteriorating, I realized that time was an issue, so I just asked, "Do you know God?" and "Who is He to you?" She told me that she knew God, but that she just never pushed the issue at home.

I did not know what to do with the information I now had, but I knew I needed to do something. I remembered the peace I received through a prayer shawl that was made for me when I went through the worst of my symptoms. I took that thought as a cue to crochet her a prayer shawl. I prayed as I crocheted, and when it was complete, I had my Order of St. Luke healing ministry pray over it. I did not expect to see Karen the day I delivered the shawl to her shop, so imagine my delight when I saw that her husband had brought her in for a visit. She had been feeling cooped up at her house and wanted a change of scenery. So her husband took her to the shop, she loved it there.

On one of my visits to Karen's house, we sat on the back porch with her husband, her brother, his wife, one of Karen's boys, and a friend. We talked about my MS, the symptoms I experienced, and how I overcame the blind invalid stage. Someone asked how I managed to get through it.

"My faith," I answered.

I only visited with Karen a couple more times. The last day I saw her, she was confined to her bed. I had a feeling it would not be much longer before she passed away, and I did not want to take time away from her family. Therefore, I made contact only through calling her shop for updates.

Another tug came on my heart. This time, it was to write two letters, one for Karen and one for her husband. These were difficult letters to write because I boldly wrote about faith, and I did not know how they would be received. Remember, in one of our earlier conversations, Karen she said she knew God, but she didn't push religion at home. To me, that meant the family didn't go to church and probably didn't talk very much about God.

I was certain that Karen knew how paramount God's role was in my healing, because I incessantly talked about it when I saw her. I hoped she could find that same peace and hope in her situation despite her dismal prognosis. I reiterated these comments in the letter to Karen and I tried to emphasize the positive impact on my life that I received from faith. Additionally, I explained that while it was personally difficult to remain positive in the darkness, I hoped she understood that a positive outlook was more for the family she was leaving behind. However, as a byproduct, she, too, could benefit.

In my letter to her husband, I explained that he could read my letter to Karen ahead of time and decide whether she could handle hearing the contents. I also thanked him for his love, and support of Karen, during a time that had to be so difficult for him. I told him my husband and I were here if he needed anything.

I mailed the letters with the intention of no more contact, no plans for personal calls to chat or visits to Karen's house or shop. In fact, I don't know whether they received the letters or if her husband ever read hers to her. A couple months later, Karen's husband called to tell me she had died and there was a memorial service planned for her if I wanted to come.

During the service, I learned that Karen had not only accepted the Lord, but she also received water baptism the month prior to her passing. After that update, I felt myself breathing in relief. I could more fully celebrate her homecoming. She was no longer suffering. After the memorial service, her husband shared with me that she used the prayer shawl daily. He said they wrapped it around her ankles to offer a cushion. I don't know the extent of my direct influence in this beautiful woman's life, but I can say she certainly added to my bucket of faith and personal growth. I believe, even for a small moment, that I was a silver lining in her life.

PHOEBE A Walker

Chapter 20
The Unexpected Move

Early in 2010, NASA officially announced that the space shuttle program was closing and mass layoffs were immanent. When Chip's boss discussed the waves of layoffs looming over his department, we took that notice as a cue to search for other employment.

Chip received two job offers. One was local, but the pay was not enough to cover our current expenses. The second offer was on the other side of the state, in Tampa. The one in Tampa appeared much better because the pay was enough to cover expenses for a rental there and our mortgage in Titusville—or so we thought.

After packing and moving to Tampa, we realized it was a mistake. We did not consider how the higher income would take us to a new income bracket, causing a significant reduction in take-home pay. Add that to a cost of living that was twice what we were paying in Titusville before the move. We ended up more upside-down financially than if Chip had taken the Titusville job.

While we were trying to wrap our minds around the income situation at the new house in Tampa, something worse came along. A rat infestation and a malfunctioning air conditioning unit. Together, they created deplorable living conditions. For health reasons, at the recommendation of a doctor, we moved out of that house and into another one after only six weeks. The cost of moving twice in two months absorbed every last dime we had and then some.

The second rental property was much more pleasant. We were renting from a physician who was super-nice. He let us paint walls and he constantly checked on us and quickly repaired issues that arose. This home was probably one of the most beautiful that I have ever lived in. So much so, that I incorporated some of the structural design to my house after we moved back to Titusville.

Good news in the middle of our chaos was that I received long-awaited news about my undergraduate college research. After two other journals turned me down, the Southeastern Association of Fish and Wildlife Agencies (SEAFWA) accepted my manuscript for publication.[10] A requirement for publishing was that I present my submission at an annual conference. I was thrilled that my persistence and prayer had finally paid off.

In October 2010, my dad and Phyllis flew into town to stay with the kids while Chip and I went off to Biloxi for the SEAFWA conference. By keeping a strong hold on Christ, I was able to walk

---

[10] Publication information is in Appendix A.

through extremely difficult life circumstances and keep a steady pace toward my goal of getting the research published.

Our move to Tampa had another positive side effect. It was the perfect opportunity for me to quit smoking. I had smoked off and on for over fifteen years. In 2008, I made the decision to quit. However, I was never able to stop smoking for much more than a couple of weeks. I started telling myself that if I could make it to a full year without smoking, I would claim a victory. I successfully quit smoking after we moved into the second house in Tampa.

My greatest struggle was the trip to Biloxi, which took place only two weeks after my quit date. The reason for my struggle was the location for presenting was in the conference area of a hotel and I had to walk through a casino to get to the conference rooms.

Picture this: I was gripping the nicotine patch on my arm super-tight, as if I were preventing it from falling off, while holding my breath and attempting to run through plumes of cigarette smoke. By afternoon, I walked slowly through the casino while attempting to suck in everyone's second-hand smoke. The next morning I was ready to yank off my patch and join the ranks of the smokers. I did not find this ordeal funny at all. However, when you ask Chip, he will tell you he was selling tickets to watch my silliness. I am happy to announce that I did not crack! In fact, I have over four years of smo-briety under my belt.

As we approached Christmas of 2010, I longed to go back to our house in Titusville. I missed our house and wished we had never moved. It probably did not help that I drove back there at least once every month just because I could. I started thinking that if we could go back to our house just for Christmas, maybe I would fulfill my desire to be there and it would be easier for me to return to Tampa. These thoughts ultimately lead to more than just visiting our house.

Looking back, I can see the necessity for moving away from our Titusville home. Two major changes occurred during that time that were imperative for my health. First, I quit smoking. The second one was regular exercise that started with walking regularly, and then I joined a gym. Before long, I was feeling healthier than I had in years.

Chapter 21

An Angel Called Robin

During Christmas of 2010, I wanted to continue our annual tradition of sharing a family dinner with friends, then going as a group to the annual Christmas parade in downtown Titusville. However, since we had moved to Tampa, we were no longer near our friends. I researched local activities in the new area. Unfortunately, I did not find a Christmas parade in close proximity. That is when I decided my family and I would return to our Titusville house. We could not afford much during this Christmas season because of the costs of moving to Tampa and the additional cost to move out of the house of horrors where we first lived. However, we had enough money to get back to our house in Titusville and stay there for the weekend.

Because our house had not yet sold, we still had utilities hooked up, and we had furniture set up for staging to help it sell. There was no need to stay at a hotel. We packed our fake Christmas tree, the kids, and the dogs and headed for home. Wayne and Carol had been friends and neighbors since we first moved to our new construction home in Titusville in May 2006. Their grandson, Brett, was the same age as our son TJ, and while Brett lived with his grandparents, the two boys hung out together.

I was so excited about returning for the weekend. The plan was for Carol to cook a fantastic meal, as she always did. Then my family would join with Jackie and Robin at Wayne and Carol's house where we would eat as a family and then head out for the Christmas parade as a group.

On the drive to our Titusville house, I tried unsuccessfully to contact Robin several times. Each time I called, I left her a message. Then I called Jackie to see if she knew anything about Robin. She said she had not heard from her, either. We figured Robin was going through one of her "I want to be by myself" moods and we did not push the issue.

On the day of the parade, Jackie drove to my house and we went to Wayne and Carol's for dinner. Jackie and I talked about stopping by Robin's trailer to check on her, but we did not want to interrupt her if she was working through something. She was the kind of person who would contact us when she was ready. We respected that and went to the parade without her. The day after the parade my family and I made the long drive back to our rental property in Tampa.

On the return trip, I attempted again to contact Robin. This was now becoming an uncharacteristically long stay away for her, especially when she had been so excited about my visit. I called Jackie and asked if she would stop by Robin's house. Because it was already very late at night, she told me she would go the next day, while she was running errands.

On Monday, Jackie went by Robin's trailer several times. One time she walked around the trailer and knocked at all the windows where she yelled, "Robin." She called me early evening to ask if she should call the police. She explained that there was only one light on in the trailer; it was the bathroom light. Jackie checked the screen door and it was locked from the inside. That meant Robin was home. The litter box on the porch was very full, which was not characteristic. Robin was meticulous about cleaning it twice a day. Another sign of trouble was that her bedroom window was open. We had just had several below-freezing days back-to-back that were record lows for us. Robin would not have left her windows open, especially not without putting a space heater on. I told Jackie that she should call the police.

Over the time, I knew Robin. When she was having serious issues that she needed help with, she called me on speed dial, and I always jumped to help her. I had talked to Robin less than a week prior to this day, and she seemed more excited about seeing me than any other time I can remember. She had recently completed several major improvements to her trailer that she was anxious to share with me. Now, no one had heard from or seen her in over four days. All of the signs around her house indicated that something was very wrong. Much more than usual. I had a feeling of dread come into my gut, much like when I learned of Ruth's death. I now feared that Robin was dead.

Even though Jackie did not smell the "smell of death" near the open window, she too felt that those signs meant Robin was either seriously injured or she had died. "Gretchen, it may be a long night," she warned me when we spoke again. I asked her to call me when the police arrived. If Robin was dead, I planned to take the two-hour drive back immediately.

Chip insisted that I should try to eat, just in case. He prepared food for me and as I was eating, Jackie called. The police had arrived and they asked her to stay back because they needed to break in. "We don't know what we'll find," they warned. Chip and I were silent as we sat awaiting confirmation of our fears. One of the officers returned outside after only a minute. He was shaking his head. Robin was in the trailer. And she was dead.

I probably shouldn't have driven then because I was very upset. However, with Robin's family living so far away, Chip, the kids, and I had become her family. How could I not have been there for her? I asked myself. I knew I needed to be with her now. Fortunately, I had not unpacked after our weekend away. I left my full plate of food on the table, grabbed my bag, added a couple things, and headed out. Two hours later, I sat outside Robin's trailer, mourning this loss. It had been ten days since we last spoke, and I already missed her. Upon reflection, I celebrated the tremendous growth in her faith walk with God, compared to when we first met. I was confident in saying she had a most amazing welcome home when she arrived at the pearly gates of Heaven.

Robin was an only child whose dad was suffering from Alzheimer's and her mom from multiple strokes. Considering their health, the news about Robin, and the weather at their home in Maryland, they could not travel or handle these end-of-life issues. Having just done this for Ruth, I was in an optimum position to assume the role. Additionally, because we had adopted Robin as part of our family, I naturally assumed the familial role with her parents. I did everything I could to help.

In spite of the cold, I offered to stay as long as I needed to. Christ knew the support I needed, and He sent specific people based on the needs of the moment. Robin passed away in her bed, and her body lay there for four days, the police estimated. One friend came on the first day to help move the mattress to the porch. She came back once more, later in the week.

I had been an active participant in the Order of St. Luke healing ministry, beginning in 2006, when I was a blind invalid. Lowell Gray was now the lead person for the group. He helped Wanda and me haul the mattress to the dump. He was perfect for that job because he was blessed with an inability to smell. Even though it was cold, the overwhelming stench of death was rancid. Every time Wanda and I felt like vomiting from the smell, he prayed for us.

Wanda was the one person who stayed with me every day through the entire event. We developed a new kind of sisterly love, as we both experienced something so deep and final together. The most emotional days for me were the ones where Jackie, Wanda, and I worked together cleaning Robin's trailer. It brought back tender memories of the Emmaus weekend we had shared with Robin.

***

Every day I kept regular contact with Robin's mom about what we were to do with various items. We separated the trash, items to donate, and important keepsakes. I did the best I could to get the most important items to her mom as quickly as possible. It was almost Christmas and it was not fair that anyone should have to deal with end-of-life details for a loved one during the Christmas season. I wanted to wade through the job as quickly as possible, so I felt I couldn't stop working long enough to sleep. By Friday, I scheduled an appointment with my former doctor because I got very sick during the clean-up process. Chip was worried and decided I should not drive home that weekend. Instead, he packed the kids and puppies and drove to our house.

At some point during the cleanup at Robin's, I found an envelope addressed to me. I cannot describe the feelings that enveloped me as I read the letter because I truly felt this message came straight from heaven. The actual writer was my beautiful friend Jackie, but it was as if Robin had given her the perfect words to write. For a moment, I felt as if I was a guest in heaven. It read:

Hi, sweet Gretchen!

I know that gas prices and tolls really bite; and still you came all the way over here because you love me and wanted to do whatever you could to help. Dear Gretchen, please fill up the truck with my compliments; it is the least I can do for someone who loves me as you do! You are the sister I never had; well, I guess you could have been my daughter from when I was really young, but the point is, you have loved me in life, and you love me enough to help my parents here in my death. I hope you can feel my love for you!

I hope you will forgive me for the horrible mistakes I have made. Please also know that I was NOT alone that night! I want you to know the Holy

Spirit was in the room with me, and, Gretchen, there really is a peace that passes all understanding! Please, dry your tears and listen to what happened to me then.

I heard a wonderful, loving voice ask me, "Robin, My Child, tell me what gives you admittance to My Father's house?" I knelt at his feet, and cried out, "Nothing but the blood of Jesus! Only by His grace can I enter." I felt a gentle hand on my head, and that sweet voice said, "THAT is the right answer, my daughter! Enter now into the glory of my Kingdom! Welcome home Robin!" Those are the best words I've ever heard!!!

Gretchen, I can't describe in words what Heaven is like; there are no human words to describe it! I just want you to know that everything Jesus said, and everything in our Bible really IS true! The glory and the beauty of this place, and the music, laughter, and love are so much more vivid than we ever can imagine on earth! I am with people I have loved, and family that have already made it here. Guess what? I saw my baby girl, and she has forgiven me! I can run, I can dance, I can leap for joy, I can do cartwheels, and I have absolutely NO PAIN! I feel stronger than I was when I was 12 years old! My smile is bigger and brighter than it has ever been --- my teeth are perfect here!

Do you remember what an awesome experience that Emmaus was for all of us? Oh Gretchen, THIS is so wonderful that it tops all that agape love. Now I can see and understand it all clearly, not as in the dark mirror of earthly experiences. And Gretchen, Jesus is the light that makes everything crystal-clear here; I have no more demons of darkness trying to strangle me and take my joy.

Do you remember that song for Easter that the choir sang at the Bridge service? Part of the words were:

No more dark, no more pain

No more tears, never crying again!

Gretchen, that is exactly my new life here in heaven! This is joy, absolute, complete, pure, untarnished Joy! Jesus explained the purpose behind my struggles and my hard times, and even the mistakes I made there. He showed me that I had been in the deep pits of pain, depression, loneliness, and alcohol and drug problems so that I could have compassion for others who were struggling and reaching out for something better. Jesus really has paid the price. Gretchen, he took me to the throne of God our Heavenly Father, and smiled as He said, "It's OK, Dad. Robin is with me!" Oh, Gretchen, this place is so wonderful and I know that you will be here to share in the joy with me some day.

In the meantime, "daughter," get out there and be a light for Christ! Remember our Emmaus promise: "Christ is counting on me, and I'm counting on Christ!" You can't see the whole picture like I can right now, but please know that if you keep your faith in Jesus and follow Him no matter what happens to you down there on earth, Jesus is going to make your life such a blessing that you will NOT believe it! The troubles we have as humans are painful and seem to last forever, but I can now tell you Gretchen, that they are just temporary --- gone in the blink of an eye! Those difficulties, if you give them to our Lord, can help you to grow and be an even stronger Ambassador of Christ. The glory that you experience here in Heaven will make you laugh at the junk you went through! Jesus IS for REAL!!!! He is absolute love and peace!"

Gretchen, please don't cry long for me. <u>Smile</u> when you remember the great times we had together, and the laughter, and the silly things I did. Please, just think of me when you see a beautiful sunrise or sunset, when you see horses galloping through a green field, and when you see sailboats cruising gently along. Think of me when you hear Jimmy Buffet singing "Margarita Ville," and when you sing "De Colores!" I will always treasure that Holy time when you sponsored me at Walk to Emmaus; it really

changed my life! I'm SO glad that I was able to be an
Ambassador for Christ!
Always feel my love, Gretchen!
Signed,
Your Robin

⁓

In Mid-January 2011, Ashley and I drove back to our house in Titusville to close on the sale of Robin's trailer. Fortunately, the sale fell through, which made it available for an old trailer park friend of Robin's, who was in a desperate situation. She did not have much money and her trailer became uninhabitable just as we were expecting more freezing weather. It felt right to sell her the trailer at a lower price than I was originally asking, something she could afford that day.

While Ashley and I were in Titusville for the sale, I took that opportunity to put together a small celebration of life for Robin. About eight people came together for this gathering. Two of the ladies were friends of Robin's from the days when she lived in the marina and they attended our church. The others who joined me were my daughter Ashley, Jackie, and Wanda, as well as Lowell and his beautiful wife Jean, who hosted the event at their house. It was beautiful to hear the various stories and see how Robin's life came full circle from her life's trials to finding salvation and peace in Christ.

I believe the fruit of patience that developed within me during my medical trials was ripe at this time. Through patience, I could exude a depth of love, forgiveness, and guidance for this fantastic woman. I do not take credit for her walk with Christ, but I believe I placed a few drops into her bucket of faith. Likewise, I feel that she too added a few drops into my bucket, which became part of a silver lining for me.

Chapter 22

Back on Track and the New Boys

In January 2011, after the trailer situation was resolved, Ashley and I felt like sticking around our house in Titusville for a bit longer. Then it crossed my mind that she had another day off from school, making it possible for us to stay yet another day, we felt the excitement. I called Chip and said, "Here's the scoop, Ashley and I, we've been talkin' and we've decided we're not coming back." Stunned but not surprised, he asked, "Do you mean forever or you're not coming back on Sunday?"

I told him we were *never* coming back.

"Negative," he said. "You will come back to get the boy child first. HA!"

Ashley and I stayed the extra day and then returned to the rental house in Tampa, where Chip and I resumed the conversation about moving back to our house in Titusville. We knew he would have to search for a new job before he could leave Tampa and move back to Titusville. It was a decision we were all willing to make sacrifices to accomplish. The kids and I returned to our house in Titusville, and

Chip made himself a geo-bachelor, where he lived with a friend in Tampa during the week and with us in Titusville on the weekends.

———

Our decision to move back to Titusville as soon as possible was an attempt to return the kids to normalcy as soon as possible. Funny, that even though we did not buy anything new during our transition, we seemed to have much more "stuff" on our return. We could not fit it all into the moving truck. Our resolution was to pack the Chevy Avalanche – vertical – and tie it down with ropes.

When we arrived back in town, Jackie was waiting in our driveway. She said we looked like "the Beverly Hillbillies returns home." The next morning, I took the house off the market and Chip began networking for a job closer to our house. Until he landed a job, we only saw him on the weekends. With his vigorous efforts, he was offered a computer science job back at Kennedy Space Center, so he rejoined us after only two months.

———

Our return to Titusville lined up perfectly with the start of my classes in February 2011. This was my original planned timing for attending seminary. When I started, I had no idea what my call was, other than I was supposed to attend classes. I loved my Spiritual Formation course, taught by Dr. Harper. By the end of that term, I believed my call was in the area of spiritual formation … or was it? It was not obvious what I could do with a degree in spiritual formation. I needed to wait for God's lead about a specific direction and purpose for this area of concentration. Starting seminary was my first legitimate attempt at setting life goals for myself that were just outside of my capability. This forced me to utilize all of my energy at attaining them.

My first term back to college coupled with reorienting the family back together after being dislocated, was a huge strain on my neurologic health. I started having issues with balance, fine motor skills, and overall functioning abilities. My health was bad enough to require IV steroids to calm my neurologic issues. This was the first time I had to go on the steroids in almost four years, and that upset me. I started asking if going to college was causing me irreversible damage. This is when God placed Sandra and Shane Shepherd on my path with a king cake.

This gesture helped me realize that I had value to someone in a time where I significantly doubted myself. Second, the cake was so full of color that it represented hope and bright future through Christ. I felt warmth, blessing, love, and cheer from that one simple gift. There are just no words to articulate the significance of this simple gesture. It meant the world to me, especially after enduring the difficult walk I had been on for the last several years. I received this as an act of love, which set me in the right mind for completing my first term at seminary. I call Shane and Sandra silver linings in my life.

Before we relocated to the rental property in Tampa, Chip and I felt a heavy tug on our hearts to adopt a middle-school aged girl. For a while, we believed the move was putting us in closer proximity to the child we would adopt. When we returned to Titusville, we felt it was time to pursue this call, and signed up for adoption classes. At the conclusion, we realized that maybe our call was not to legally adopt a child, because we were not having any luck finding a good match in the adoption community. However, because we had two kids, there were always teenagers in and out of our house. The classes prepared us to bring teens under our wings and love them into the right direction. That is what we did.

We added two boys to our family through love, not the judicial system, because they were over the legal age of eighteen. The first young man was Brett Ricks, Wayne and Carol's grandson. The second young man was Ryan Wensel. Both of my kids and Brett knew Ryan from the Junior ROTC at the high school. My kids were excited to have them join our family because they had always wanted more siblings. It also meant that there were more individuals to share chores.

I believe these two young men found something in our family that they needed. Both became at least part-time residents in our house when we invited them in at the end of January 2013.

Brett's reputation was that of a bully—but, like a Chihuahua, he was all bark and no bite. He ran his mouth and when it came time to follow through with the actions to support his words, there were none. It always seemed like he was trying to protect himself from deeper hurts. He yearned to be the center of attention, as a sign of acceptance, and did not feel like he received it from many people. Unfortunately for Brett, once he found himself in a situation where things were going very good, he always managed to sabotage his success and found himself hurting and having to start over.

Brett was living with his grandparents as he headed into his last term of high school, in the spring of 2013. By this point, he had created a reputation for himself with teachers, students, and the administration that threatened to keep him from graduating. This was a culmination of not turning in assignments, being disrespectful to teachers and administration, and running his mouth with students. His grandparents could handle doing all that was necessary to get him to graduation, but their jobs' peak season was in the spring, which directly corresponded with Brett's last term in high school.

Chip and I offered to take him in for that last term to help him tackle this major hurdle. We spent hours of one on one time with Brett to help him with his academics. We also made multiple trips to the high school to meet with teachers and administrators, to resolve issues whether from not doing assignments or his attitude towards others. By the end of the term, Brett was completing all of his assignments. He even put his behavior in check, at least as well as he could. Ultimately, he did what he needed to successfully complete high school.

When we brought Ryan into our house at the end of January 2013, he was looking for direction. He moved in during the same term we were helping Brett. It was the last term in school for all three of us. Ryan quickly showed us he was extremely self-sufficient and capable of motivating himself. His main need was to have time to be a kid without heavy pressures, and he needed to learn how to focus, by burning off some youthful energy and desires in order to start focusing on his future. After moving into our house, he picked up two part-time jobs and bought a vehicle. After graduation, he went to a recruiter and joined the service.

During the spring of 2013, my house was hopping busy. Of the six people under my roof, we never knew who was coming, going, turning around, or upside down. I LOVED it, because when things got bad, they did not fester long enough to feel the full impact before things turned amazing. We took the time to celebrate everything.

That May, on the very same day, the boys and I made it to graduation. My commencement was in the morning, theirs was that evening, and the next day we had a full-blown luau bash to celebrate our accomplishments. Eleven days later, I celebrated my fortieth birthday. As the dust settled from these extreme high events, the Lord reconnected me with Cristi, who began planning a visit to my house for the next month.

While there were great difficulties during this stage of life, I believe there were equal amounts of personal growth and celebrations of major accomplishments. Because we could not take this pivotal yet chaotic life walk in our own strength, we leaned heavily on God's love, grace, and mercy. He sent many tools and silver linings. I won't say they made the walk easy, but they certainly made it possible.

Chapter 23

A Living Angel Named Jennilee

The military had moved us all over since I was married the first time in 1994. After I married Chip in 1997, the military moved us several more times. Then, in 2001, when Chip switched from active duty to reserve status with the military, we moved again in search of the right climate to help me with my disease. It was finally time to settle down in May 2006, when we moved into our newly constructed house. We had no intentions of moving out of our house before both TJ and Ashley graduated from high school.

⌐───────────⌐

The darkest days with my MS occurred shortly after we moved into our house in 2006. Because the kids were only starting to develop friendships, their new friends did not see repercussions from these dark MS trials. This spared them from seeing how scary bad the disease really was. However, as time rolled forward, several of their friends saw micro-glimpses of my symptoms. Either they came to visit when I was in the middle of an exacerbation and they saw my inability to do things properly, or they saw me with the IV during treatment. On those occasions, though, they could see that I was managing the disease quite well, not so scary.

In the four years between moving into our new construction home in Titusville and our move to Tampa, our kids had developed strong bonds with their friends. We had fully anticipated that they would develop their best relationships ever in Titusville. While TJ was very introverted and had only a few friends, they were among his best friends ever. These boys did not participate in school functions; they spent most of their time as homebodies, playing video games. Ashley, on the other hand, was quite active with school and her friends. Chip and I dearly loved all of her friends and their parents. It was as if we all became part of the same family. In fact, when the girls had school functions and award ceremonies, all the parents sat together to cheer them on. The parents became the girls' biggest cheerleaders—that was a textbook picture of a village raising the children.

It was difficult for my family to make the move to Tampa. We were all so tired of moving and had finally lived in a house longer than three years. What would happen to the relationships we had created? Would they remain after we moved? We looked for ways to reduce the hardship of a move—especially for Ashley because she was in middle school, the worst time to move with a teenaged girl.

In an attempt to help Ashley adjust to the move, we brought a couple of her friends with us to Tampa when we went to sign our rental agreement. This way, the girls could see the house we were moving into and help leave behind some happy memories for Ashley. Unfortunately, the strain this move had on my health caused the girls to experience the ugly side of my disease.

We arrived at the Tampa house in July 2010 for our walk through. Even though this was the hottest time of the year, the realty company left the air-conditioning off. I figured I would be okay if we were not there too long. An hour later, we were finally done with the walk through and heading over to the management office to sign the documents. That office also did not have the air conditioning turned on and the building was very hot. We explained to the realtor that I had MS and the heat was very bad for me. We asked if he could put the air conditioning on. He said no, that he would make this quick. For the record, it was not quick; I have never signed so many documents for a rental property before.

My vision became blurry and it was difficult to hold the pen. I told Chip that I was scared, I felt trapped, as if something bad was about to happen, and I could do nothing to stop it. I got up from the table and walked into the hallway looking for cooler air. Just as I stepped out of the room, I collapsed onto the floor. Chip rushed to scoop my unresponsive body off the floor and ran with me to the truck, where he blasted cold air conditioning on me. He also acquired a ten-pound bag of ice and wrapped my arms around it, to cool my core body temperature.

There we were in a crisis situation, Chip was ready to take me to the Emergency Room, and we had two of Ashley's friends with us. Thoughts of how scared the girls must be as they watched this happen raced through my head, but I could do nothing to change the situation. I remember praying that God would help me so that we wouldn't have to go to the hospital. I just wanted to get home. Fortunately, Chip's quick thinking and the cooling measures helped me in time. We decided I did not need to go to the hospital and we returned the girls safely to their homes in Titusville.

That was just one example of a couple friends watching the scary neurologic beast. So, what happens when one of them experiences her own scary neurologic beast? The girls were in the second term of sophomore year in high school, spring 2012, when Jennilee started having issues alarmingly similar to my own. Jennilee is a bubbly high-spirited young lady, packed into a super small body and she has high aspirations of becoming the next great Steven Spielberg. Imagine the fears she had about her future when she woke up one morning with odd skin sensations that covered her body and an inability to use her right hand. In her stubbornness, she decided to go to school and work through it. After doing this for a week, her mom decided Jennilee needed medical attention. The doctor said everything looked fine and sent her home. "You just need more sleep," he advised.

When her mom explained her symptoms to me, I remember thinking they sounded a great deal like my own neurologic symptoms. My gut rolled at the idea that one of my daughter's friends could also have MS. I told Jennilee's mother that while they sounded like my symptoms, there could be so many other causes. "Just give it some time," I suggested.

But Jennilee continued having issues with her hand, preventing her from taking the abundant notes she needed. The frustrations convinced her mom to take her back to the doctor. This time he started running tests on her. The MRI revealed one lesion in her brain. Yes, she had only one lesion and one neurologic episode. However, to have a diagnosis of multiple sclerosis, the scan needed to reveal multiple lesions. Additionally, an MS diagnosis requires two separate neurologic episodes affecting two different areas of the body, each separated by time. This was not the case with Jennilee, so the doctor sent her home saying, "We will continue to watch this." After three weeks, the symptoms went away.

During the summer 2013, Jennilee and her family spent an entire week at the beach in the sun. By the end of the week, Jennilee was not feeling well. She had intense pain in her skin and when it was touched, it felt as if her skin was seared. Clothing, hair, necklaces, wind, anything that touched her skin, evoked that same response. By the end of the day, a new one replaced that symptom. She felt the sensation of needles in her feet. By morning, this sensation covered her body from her feet to her shoulders. Her stomach felt as if it was sticking a mile out, bloated, and Jennilee's mind felt disoriented. She went to her parents in tears, concerned and scared.

"She needs to be admitted. Bring her in now, so we can run more tests," doctors ordered, when Jennilee's parents called them. The MRI revealed two more lesions in her brain. Now they could diagnose her with MS, and start her on intravenous steroids to reduce the inflammation in her brain. The timing of her admittance to the hospital corresponded with the IV infusion that I was receiving after I completed graduate school in the summer of 2013.

Jennilee was hospitalized for a full week on IV steroids before her symptoms started to wane. They completely subsided after she returned home and was weaned off the steroids. During her week in the hospital, she and I spent time chatting with each other through Facebook and texts. In this way, I did what I could to lift her spirits. I hoped she could see that we were a team fighting the same battle together, with God as our captain.

Jennilee is a very strong young lady, and she is going to keep living in spite of this diagnosis. She continues to go to school and does all she can to stay as active and "normal" as she possibly can. Sometimes people want to do things for her, others want to make things easier for her, and yet she just wants life to remain the same as it was before the diagnosis. I believe she can have a similar life as long as she continues doing what she can while she can.

Since her diagnosis, Jennilee reminded me about how inspiring my life with MS has been for her new walk. "I remember looking up to you, because even though it was clear to see that MS could be very challenging and so demolishing to both your will and your spirit, Miss Gretchen, there you were, still smiling and facing life hand in hand with God," she said. "I loved seeing that. Even in your worst times, I saw how you turned the negative situation around to praise God. Now I believe that no matter what I face, even if it is not the same magnitude, if you can do it, if you can turn a horrid situation around for the glory of God, then I certainly can too."

She added, "I remember you telling me if I was diagnosed with MS, it was going to be okay. When the diagnosis came, and I learned I was stricken with the very same disease you dealt with, you became the angel on my doorstep. I will be honest, I was very frightened, not knowing what having MS was going to mean for me, but watching you helped me so much. I looked at you with a new understanding. I learned that having an episode from MS can be so terrible, just utterly debilitating in every way. However, even when you were having an episode, you were still doing everything you wanted... sure, some days you struggled but you didn't let MS stop you from enjoying the things you love in life. It was from that moment that I stopped fearing my disease. I knew if you could handle it, then so could I. Through Christ who strengthens us, all things are possible. Miss Gretchen, you were the perfect example of that."

Jennilee spoke about the peace I gave her mom, who, I knew, was so upset she felt like her world would not quit spinning. They both saw me as someone who understood and could help them walk through this new life walk. Jennilee said, "I believe God allowed this cross for me to bear, and I will carry it to honor Him. Miss Gretchen, you helped me to get the acceptance I have today. I don't fear my disease, the possibility of going blind, or of not being able to walk. I don't fear the medication I give myself every week. I don't fear tomorrow, because I know that no matter how hard it gets, no matter what MS throws at me, God is there with me every single step of the way. Then, when it is too much for my flesh and bone to handle, when the tears are streaming down my cheeks because I cannot dress myself, or apply my own makeup, I stop, take a deep breath, and remind myself that God is standing with me and strengthening me. It was you, Miss Gretchen, from the beginning, who helped me get this attitude and acceptance. So, thank you!"

This young lady thinks I am very strong. She makes me feel like a super hero! I thank the Lord for crossing our paths because while I am almost halfway through my life walk, she is merely at the beginning. I cannot put words to the effect I have had on her life, but I am so grateful I was able to be that light, silver lining for her.

I pray to God, that the inspiration she found in me is enough to keep her forward momentum. Jennilee is immensely intelligent, and she has great plans for going to college and becoming a movie director. This walk for her includes a rather large cross to bear. Many of her peers will not understand, yet I believe she will persevere to culmination of all her efforts. She will be a shining star all on her own, for so many others she has yet to meet.

The same week, in June 2013, when Jennilee and I were receiving intravenous steroids for our MS episodes, we both had friends walking with us. For me, this is when God sent Cristi to my house and she personally drove me to the infusion center.

Chapter 24

God Re-connects Me with Cristi

Out of the ashes of my past, in 2013, God found a way to reconnect Cristi and me after ten years of separation. Even in those years apart, I thought of her often. Every time I was in desperation and looking for God, I was thankful Cristi had helped me invite Christ into my heart that night in her room. All those years ago, when I was sixteen, God sent me to her house for a reason. Now He was sending her to my house.

When we got on the phone with each other, Cristi said that she truly believed God wanted her to come to my house for an extended stay. God laid a message on my heart: that Cristi was going through her own walk in the valley. Even before she talked about coming to my house, I felt that something was guiding her to me, and that I was supposed to stay clear of the reasons. No anticipations.

God knew that I was actively involved in three very different churches and with Order of St. Luke healing ministry at two different churches. My plan was to let Cristi come to my house and gain exposure to everything I was doing, so that God could guide her heart in the way he wanted to.

She arrived at my house a month after the three graduations (two high school and my graduate school), just in time for my next round of IV steroids. The timing was awesome. Chip let Cristi take me to the infusion center and hang out for the long hours of infusion. We were able to catch up on lost time, how our lives had squirrelled around. Best of all, she shared her experience in the Holy Land. As she sat next to me sharing the pictures, I felt like I had touched the Holy soil with her.

At the infusion center, Cristi experienced some of the same joys I do at that place—yes, I am being facetious. The bottom line is that I have choices: I could go to that place and cry my eyes out because it sucks as bad as it does, or I could intentionally seek humor. And humor is my favorite thing to find.

When I am on the IV steroids, especially at the beginning, there is entirely too much humor to experience. The ladies who work there are awesome and they seem to enjoy the humor that follows me into that building. What was it they once told me? Oh, "You never know what you are going to get when Gretchen comes through the door."

I have gone to the IV infusion center enough times to develop a pattern. It goes like this… When I walk through the door, I see Ollie at the front desk. She is a no-nonsense woman who is full of spirit. I always stop by to let her know I am there, say good morning, and tell her how beautiful she is. Then Ollie tells me what room number is mine. I take my purse, jacket, and drink to the room and set it on my chair. On the way to the bathroom, I say hello to my two regular nurses, Jeannine and Sylvia. By the time I return to my chair, either Ollie or the nurses have guided whoever is with me, usually Chip, to my room.

After I return to my chair, I sign admission papers and have vital signs taken. Then everyone in the room with me bows their heads so I can pray over God's will for the medication and my symptoms. My nurse gets the IV in place, and we start treatment. This time, June 2013, Cristi was my support person.

Okay, so day one of the steroids, my room was directly across the hall from the bathroom. Cristi had been sharing pictures with me of her trip to the Holy Land in Israel. I knew I had to go to the bathroom, but was so excited about her pictures that I just held it. That was a big mistake, because once I realized I could not wait any longer, I was afraid I would not make it across the hall before my bladder popped. Cristi decided to stay in my room while I took my IV pole on walkabout to the bathroom. This maneuver was skewed as my lower body stayed to the left, along with my butt, while I intentionally pushed my upper body in the opposite direction, towards the rest room.

My plan was to correct the misdirected lower part of my body. By this point, I was making a lot of noise because I could not coordinate my IV pole with my body's actions. The pole and my upper body went in one direction, while my lower body went the opposite. The noise I was making while trying to control my body's split mentality had attracted an audience. Sylvia, one of my two fabulous nurses, managed to both catch and then push my tail end in the correct direction before I smashed into a wall. My body became correctly oriented just as I reached the bathroom door, when I felt my shoulder slightly clip the edge of the doorframe. But, victory! I was in the bathroom and I had did not experience leakage. Hallelujah and praise God!

When the time came to return to my room, I stood in the open door of the bathroom and contemplated the situation. "It's only about six or seven good sized steps between the bathroom door and my chair. If I just hold my breath and go real fast, I should be able to get from here to there without the same issues I had on the way to the bathroom." Okay, one … two … three … I held my breath and went for it. STEP-step.step.step.step … THUD … Ka-BLAMB! With that speed, I had excellent momentum to throw myself against the wall while completely missing the threshold of my door.

The problem was that my legs were still off, which oriented my stride to the left, causing me to miss the door completely. Instead, that whole physics momentum theory kicked in. My short quick steps rapidly propelled me forward until my IV pole hit the wall and I kept going until I smashed into both the IV pole and the wall.

Jeannine, my other fantastic nurse, and Cristi had the comical view as they saw me standing in the bathroom door and watched me prepare to come across. Then, in the blink of an eye, I was not there … followed by the crash. This lead to a mad dash to my aid, where they found me dazed from impact. I only momentarily felt defeated, realizing that my execution had failed so miserably. No matter, there were not many dry eyes, thanks to the laughter, including my own.

It sure feels good to find humor in situations that have the potential to be so dark. In this case, I had the added benefit of sharing this experience with Cristi. Now when I have to return to the infusion center, as I already have several times since she was there with me, I have fond memories to reflect on. I did not have an awkward moment with Cristi at the infusion center; it just felt like the right thing in the perfect time.

During Cristi's two-week stay, she experienced the crazy chaos of my house, between my schedule and all those young adult people we had onboard with us. I did everything I could not to interject thoughts about what we were doing and where we were going. I made every effort to make sure she got to experience it all.

One night, my newest friend, Tammy, invited us to her church. She said there was a special healing event taking place and God tugged on her heart to invite Cristi and me. Tammy and I both thought that the invitation was more for Cristi than us, since He had sent her all the way from Indiana to Florida. "In the name of making sure you experience everything, maybe we should go," I told Cristi. She agreed.

There I was, standing in between Cristi and Tammy, one of my oldest and one of my newest friends. We were sing-sing-singing praises when my legs started to feel like spaghetti under me. The Spirit was powerfully strong in that place. I thought to myself, "Girl, you are NOT going down!" Then one of the church pastors, Rita, walked up to me, took my hand, and walked me to the front, where people were actively praying with each other.

Rita leaned over me and spoke intimate details about my past, specifically my mother and my need to forgive her. But, by the grace of God, she could not have known those things; she did not know me from Adam. I went back to my seat and cried hard. When I calmed down, I stood up and began singing again.

Finally, our guest speaker was introduced. He was there to do a healing service – something I was a little skeptical about, although, I told myself, if anyone was healed from it, then great. He asked, "Is there anyone here suffering from a disease, who wants healing?" Of course, I raised my hand. I had been asking God to take this thorn from me for years.

There was Cristi sitting next to me in all of her excitement, she was aggressively pointing both of her index fingers at me. I just knew he was going to address *me* first–and there he was, walking towards me from the opposite side of this huge sanctuary to where he stopped – right next to me. He asked what my name was and inquired about the disease.

He took me by the hand and walked me to the front of the church, and I thought, "Uh-oh, here we go again, back to the front of the church." I warned myself, "Girl, listen to me. We are staying off the floor—remember that."

When we reached the front of the sanctuary, he took my other hand and began to pray aloud. As he prayed, my legs turned into spaghetti. However, I was NOT going to hit the floor at this church that was not my own! It took every effort I had to prevent myself from dropping to the floor like a heavy anvil. When he finished praying, I could not find words on my tongue to speak. However, I immediately recognized I had clearer vision. On the return to my seat, I stared around the room in amazement. I saw things I had not been able to see minutes before.

The focus of the event was on healing; you were either praying for healing or you were receiving prayer for healing. I had already received my prayer for healing. Now I wanted to focus on giving thanks to God and praying for the healing of others.

While I was standing with my arms in the air, my legs began to give out. The seats in the sanctuary were like those in a movie theater; they spring closed when no one is sitting in them. I thought, if I stick my rear end out far enough and just drop, then I could catch myself on the edge of the seat and prevent my butt from hitting the floor. I successfully executed the plan.

Now that I was on the edge of the chair, I felt heavy, as if the floor was still calling my name. I thought to myself, "Okay, maybe if I drape my upper body over the seat in front of me, it will lock me in place, preventing further descent to the floor." As soon as I parked my head in the crook of my arm, a complete stranger approached me.

She leaned over the top of me and said, "I am not a member of this church, but God told me to stop by and tell you …" I can't remember exactly what she said but I know that it deeply touched my heart.

What in the world? God had my number that night for sure. I had agreed to attend this function believing it was for Cristi. But now I was starting to wonder. I had not really thought of much more that night than keeping my butt off the floor – that same floor that refused to stop calling me.

Something about that stranger bringing a message from God made me realize I could no longer contain my emotions. There was a level of love and healing in the church that no words can accurately articulate. I cried so hard I could almost not breathe. I had so many tears and the mucous that literally hung from my nose to the floor. Under normal circumstances, I might have been embarrassed. However, my energy was already spent on keeping my dang butt off the floor.

Unbeknownst to me, Tammy and Cristi had been watching my progression and as they chuckled at me. They came into agreement that

I should just go to the floor. Cristi said, "Wouldn't it just be easier to go to the floor?" then Tammy added, "You should just let yourself go."

Something about those words sounded good. I was now sitting on the aisle, so I eased myself out and just slightly to the side, where only my butt was on the floor and I was hanging onto the arm. Then Tammy firmly said, "Just let gooooooooo and allow God to do His work." The moment I lifted my head and let go of the arm of the seat, BAM. I hit the floor. HARD.

I landed in a distorted pretzel-like position that I could not undo. I was lying there thinking how odd it felt. I could not move or speak and the room felt like it would not stop moving. Yes, I knew what was happening had to be from God. I spoke to Him in my head, and said, "I know you are doing something in me. This feels weird and I don't like it, but I trust that you are doing something good in me, so thank you. I love you so much! Thank you." I just kept thanking God. After a bit, I opened my eyes to see a stranger standing over me, I think it was Rita but I can't remember. I checked, and nope, I still could not talk or move. So I shut my eyes again.

After some time passed, Tammy and Cristi thought they needed to call Chip to come get us because I was the one who had driven there. Fortunately, however, I started moving on my own again. I did not fully understand what happened that night, but I knew it had to be something good.

⁓

When the time came for Cristi to return home, she was much more affectionate than the day she arrived. The day I picked her up at the airport, she was standoffish about giving me a hug. By the time she went home, she was hugging and saying, "I love you" to everyone. She said she truly felt blessed to have visited and was not ready to go back home.

The good news was that she went home a changed woman. What I knew before Cristi came was that she had something personal going on in her life that she believed God wanted to work on. She felt God called her to come to my house for an extended stay. In this way, she could separate herself from her daily activities and contacts and open her eyes to Him at the various churches I participated.

On that visit, in 2013, Cristi experienced four different types of church services (a non-denominational service Chip and I were helping to start up, Tammy's non-denominational church, my Methodist church, and my Episcopalian church). My Order of St. Luke Healing ministry took place at both the Episcopal and Methodist churches. Add to that the crazy chaotic life in my house with different schedules for six people.

After arriving back home in Indiana, Cristi told me she regularly reflected on her time at my house. She mostly remembered how many people were in my house and how we were able to keep everyone's schedule straight. To this day, she tells me that one of the first things she recognized was how much of a matriarch I was in the house. The people scheduled their activities around my abilities and schedule, and I was the one who led household prayer regularly. In this house, dinners were at the table and that is where our regular communication took place. Outside of my house, she gleaned a great deal from my various religious affiliations, specifically Order of St.

Luke healing ministry and the Episcopal Church. She allowed these experiences and connections to help her create a new life for herself and a more fulfilling relationship with God when she returned home to Indiana.

The visit was not solely for Cristi's sake. We both benefited. Something about her visit gave me a sensation of completeness. I don't understand why, I just know the feeling. Neither Cristi nor I could have accomplished this on our own, but through our desire and effort to be obedient to Christ, it was possible. I believe there is no substitute for power that comes when we utilize the entire body of Christ, especially with respect to trials. I am so thankful I said yes to Cristi coming to stay during that time. I feel more complete in Christ through this experience.

Chapter 25

Where to From Here?

Clearly, my life path has taken me through many tremendous highs and lows. How can I top them? Do I attempt to?

No, I think they are simply what they are: stepping-stones to the creation of the person I am today. While I have had horrific trials, as difficult as it is to say, I would not deny any of them. It seems that the greater the trial I walked through, the greater the fulfillment and reward on the other side. Additionally, the various walks I have taken have opened opportunities for me to offer hope and inspiration to others going through similar situations. I find some of my greatest satisfaction in life comes from walking with those going through similar hardships. I personally found it much easier to walk through a trial with someone who understands, because they knew the right things to say and do, and could offer guidance, and hope.

Earlier in the book, I talked about my desires to study biology and to attend seminary. However, they do not totally encompass the woman I am. Nor do they offer a precise direction for my future. In fact, I do not believe I can determine my future without considering all the details that define me. I am a mother with only one chick-ling still in the roost. I feel complete when I am able to do many things at once: utilize my creative side, draw on my intellectual side, and serve as an inspiration to others, especially my husband and kids. Maybe this multi-faceted persona *IS* an indicator of my purpose and direction.

***

Separate from what I do in life is who I will be in this world. My deepest desire is to find heaven here on earth. In my definition, that means a place where people do not oppose each other. Rather, they join in a mutual cause, to live the best physical life they can. I believe we accomplish this by treating all humanity as equals. After all, we share a creator.

I imagine that my love for people is the reason I enjoy cruises so much. The people who work onboard a ship do so side-by-side with people they would not otherwise associate with because of their countries' laws. Those are human-created boundaries. The people who cruise have the opportunity to leave the stresses of life at home and allow themselves downtime to relax. Through this, they are not so hard on themselves and they become capable of sharing familial love with complete strangers. I believe this exudes the perfect picture of our spiritual design and a personal desired purpose.

***

My trials were both large and difficult. The concept that helped me to walk through them was the realization that hard times will come in life. None of us is exempt, and we should not want to be. By design, trials are part of our lives and elements necessary to make our personal stories full and complete. Maybe my largest challenge should not be getting through these times, but focusing on how I will celebrate each of the trials I have survived.

⌒——⌒

As for direction, I do not need to know a physical destination. We should not attempt to see farther than what the present light illuminates. God never intended for us to see the entire picture right now.

I have MS, but it does not define who I am, and what I can or cannot do. More simply, I look at it as the cross I bear. I am still functional, though at times I need to lean on other people or devices to have that ability. As long as I remember to keep my cross at the forefront of my mind, I believe God will provide the crutches—the silver linings—that I need to do His will.

⌒——⌒

I believe sharing my story is the best place to start. As for the technical decisions about career, I will just go where the wind—God—sends me. If it is a position in the field of biology, I will take it. Likewise, if it is a spiritual/theological position, I will take that.

I imagine there will be seasons for both.

Now that I have shared where I have been, who I am, and who I aim to become, I want to conclude with this final thought on God's call for me. It is highly probable, thanks to the number and magnitude of trials I have walked through, that God's call is for me to share my plethora of stories through motivational speaking. I believe it may help people find hope after hearing about how one person survived—and flourished—through difficult times. My stories stress that I could not and did not find success on my own. God was always with me, and so were helpful strangers and great friends—my silver linings.

In fact, as I reflect on what I have written, I realize another common thread originated in the consequences of my abuse. It started in my early years, when I was exposed to things a girl of my age should not experience. The abuse led to irrational thinking, which manifested itself into bad behavioral choices. That promiscuity led to the pregnancies at a young age that caused me to mature more quickly into an adult without fully developing through my juvenile stages.

Once I started having children, my heart's desire was to have several girls. Perhaps that was because I wanted to re-do my youth by living vicariously through daughters. I could give them everything I lacked, while protecting them from harm, I thought. When Chip and I went to adopt, the age group that we requested was a girl between the ages of seven and fifteen. An epiphany came to me while I was writing this section. I was seven years old when my parents divorced, and I was fifteen when I moved in with my dad. I don't believe that choice of an age range was a coincidence.

The next point in this thread occurred during my time at seminary, as I was attempting to decipher God's call for my life. I felt a strong call to help teenaged moms by developing a crisis pregnancy center. My personal experience with teenage pregnancies and what led up to those pregnancies was a discipleship moment waiting to happen. I wanted to talk to girls and help them realize the truth of their situations. In this way, they could see that they were wonderful and beautiful in God's eyes, and they had a purpose. When I learned there was already a crisis pregnancy center in Titusville, I conceded that might not be God's plan for me.

Now, while reading the finished product of this book, I see that I have the necessary tools be a motivational speaker, to help build up and encourage people, especially young females. That could be the direction the wind—God's wind—is blowing me. Regardless, I will try not to put a label on my direction. I will just show up to God's desk and await my new orders. After all, I am only at my best when He is in the driver's seat.

Epilogue

I am starting to forget the exact feeling I had in the very moment I first felt the angel sitting next to me, in the living room, during some of my darkest days. I continue to be humbled by the deep feeling of a divine spirit in my direct presence that day in 2006. Please don't misunderstand. I do not want to be back in that place again in order to feel it. I know it will come again when it is time for me to take my ascent to heaven. The wonderful part of the moment was that I was able to experience the divine presence, and in such, I have a constant reminder to stay on the path. Once you have experienced something so holy, nothing else on this earth can match its majesty, beauty and power. NOTHING!

While reading this book, I am sure you noticed a common process: tragedy happened, I wondered what caused it and if it would get better, I asked where God was, God presented Himself to me, and offered tools—my silver linings or angels—to move me forward. As the title "Encounters with Angels" indicates, I believe those people were sent directly from God to carry me through trials, or they were placed here for me to walk with them through their trials.

In each situation, just when I thought no one was there, we had a pouring out from the Order of St. Luke, Emmaus, and the

Discipleship communities. All of these angels were God with skin on. Now that I know where to look, I do not have an excuse to stay down when things get difficult—and getting up is the key!

Because of the fall in the Garden of Eden, trials will plague our lives. Some will be our personal trials; others will be trials we watch happen to those we love. In these times, we can expect to be crushed and broken. The only way to put the pieces back is to go to the master potter; he takes the broken pieces and makes them beautiful. The song, "The Broken Beautiful," by Ellie Holcomb, articulates this concept well.

Recently, I talked to my daughter about how badly it felt to be broken and crushed. She said, "Mom, think about how the most intense pressure creates a diamond. Once the diamond is created, it is very solid and virtually impossible to crush. Maybe if we think of our trials as creation of diamonds, we can hold out through that refiner's fire long enough to become that beautiful diamond. Diamonds are attractive to look at and bright enough to illuminate."

I love how God speaks to me through my daughter!

Regardless of the roller coaster of emotions my life walk has influenced me through, I must remind myself that I am always a victor in Christ, not a victim. Sometimes things just happen, and whether we are in a tough life walk or under attack, physical or perceived, we need to trust that no matter how bleak or desperate our situation appears to be, God IS there with us!

Our attitudes and responses to our current life situations play a tremendous role in our response. For instance, in the moments when I felt like a victim, I displayed some hefty emotional diarrhea. The moment I found God's face again, I put on His armor and gained a strength that could take mighty creatures—and problems—down. No matter what we are living with, it is our decision to choose a response.

I choose life—it's worth fighting for!

Appendix A

My Research Site:

www.seafwa.org

Search proceedings under publications

For – Gretchen E. Walker **(case sensitive)**

My Surfboard location:

Madd Jacks Grillin Shack

Cocoa Beach, FL

www.maddjacksgrillinshack.com

APPENDIX B

Breast Cancer Links I used:

1. National Breast Cancer Foundation, Inc. - http://www.nationalbreastcancer.org/

2. National Breast Cancer Foundation, Inc. Donations - https://www.nationalbreastcancer.org/breast-cancer-donations

3. Susan G. Komen Breast Cancer Foundation - http://ww5.komen.org/

4. The Center for Restorative Breast Surgery (Where surgeons performed my double mastectomy and reconstruction)- http://www.breastcenter.com/

5. 1717 St. Charles Avenue New Orleans, LA 70130 | Tel: 504.899.2800 | Fax: 504.899.2700 | Toll Free: 888.899.2288| info@breastcenter.com

Multiple Sclerosis:

1. National Multiple Sclerosis Society - http://www.nationalmssociety.org/
2. For donations to the Multiple Sclerosis society - http://www.nationalmssociety.org/Donate
3. Dr. Scott Gold (My neurologist) - http://scottlgold.md.com/ 321-725-4500

   1223 Gateway Drive Suite 2G, Melbourne, FL 32901
   and
   7125 Murrell Road Suite F, Melbourne, FL 32940

Lou Gehrig's Disease:

Lou Gehrig's ALS Association – http://www.alsa.org/about-als/what-is-als.html

---

Churches:

1. Indian River City United Methodist Church (IRC)

    www.ircumc.com

    1355 Cheney Hwy, Titusville, FL 32780 – Phone: (321) 267-7922

2. St. Gabriel's Episcopal Church

    www.stgabriels.church

    414 Pine St, Titusville, FL 32796 –Phone: (321) 267-2545

Chiropractor/Acupuncturist:

Daly Integrated Medical Group

http://dalyimg.com/

2708 Garden St, Titusville, FL 32796 · (321) 267-4324

Appendix C

Vow renewal

WEDDING PROGRAM
March 24th, 2007

---

1. Three sounds from the conch shell:

This marks the beginning of the ceremony and signifies the presence of the holy trinity.

2. Lei exchange:

A Hawaiian wedding often begins with the lei exchange for several different reasons.

One is that the Lei is a circle, like the rings that are worn representing the eternal commitment and unbroken devotion of your hearts to each other.

Another is that each individual flower that is woven into the Lei loses none of its individual beauty when it forms the circle. Its beauty is enhanced. Likewise, in your marriage you do not compromise or lose your individual identity and unique beauty.

3. Opening

4. Vows

5. Exchange of rings

- Wait, we've already done that, so we are going to do two other ceremonies instead.

First will be a blessing of our hands, followed by a lasso ceremony. The lasso is draped in a figure 8 around our wrists by the pastor signifying eternity of our love and marriage. This ceremony will conclude with a recommitment to our marriage.

6. Unity candle time

Ok, so we can't light candles on a windy beach. In its place, we chose to do a sand ceremony. From this day forward, we will have this beautiful sand jar to remind us about how beautifully we blend.

7. Conclusion including wreath ceremony…

We will remove the leis that we have been wearing and carry them to the ocean. Tradition says that if we take them to the ocean and offer them out to our deceased relatives/friends, when they come back, we, as the happy couple, will have received the blessing of those deceased relatives/friends. We will also perform a wreath ceremony at this time. We take a wreath, which represents trials, hurts, failures, etc. of our time together and offer them up to God by sending the wreath out to sea. Tradition says that when the wreath comes back, we've been cleansed of all those hard times/trails, hurts, failures, etc. Then we get to kiss again… YAY! Then you all, our guests, may go upstairs to the reception room while we clean up the beach and take photos.

Mahalo nui loa na ho'olaule'a me la kaua. Ua ola loko I ke aloha.
(Thank you for celebrating with us. Love gives life within.)

The Service:

Blow in the conch shell three times (signifying the presence of the holy trinity) then the pastor will say a prayer.

Pastor hand Chip a lei to place on Gretchen with a kiss and hand Gretchen a lei to place on Chip with a kiss.

OPENING:

(Brenda) Good relationships never stop growing. Like fine wine, they get better with age. Chip and Gretchen, you have now been married for ten years, and through all of the years of your journey together, you have now come to this beautiful setting, so that you can renew your vow and commitment of love for each other.

No marriage is perfect. As you continue in this union, you already know that it will continue to take a lot of love and work to keep your relationship an ongoing success. Many couples tend to think of marriage as a 50/50 proposition. Actually, the best relationships are 90/10. If you both will give 90% and take only 10%, you will have a formula likely to continue to bring both of you happiness for a lifetime.

As you continue on your journey together, I ask you to remember this advice:

- Let your love be stronger than your anger.
- Learn the wisdom of compromise, for it is better to bend than to break.
- Believe the best of your beloved rather than the worst.
- Confide in your partner and ask for help when you need it.
- Remember that true friendship is the basis for any lasting relationship. Give your spouse the same courtesies and kindnesses you bestow on your friends. Say, "I love you" every day.

Chip and Gretchen, I remind you that marriage is a precious gift, a lifelong dedication to love and a daily challenge to love one another more fully and more freely.

With this understanding, do you Chip, continue to take Gretchen as your beloved wife? Will you continue to be a tender faithful husband, continue to love and cherish her, in sickness and health, for richer, for poorer, for better, for worse, and keep yourself only unto her?

With this understanding, do you Gretchen, continue to take Chip as your beloved husband, continue to love and cherish him, in sickness and health, for richer, for poorer, for better, for worse, and keep yourself only unto him?

VOWS:

(Pastor) say a prayer.

Eternal God, creator and preserver of all life, author of salvation, giver of all grace, bless Chip and Gretchen, who come now to recommit themselves in holy marriage. Grant that they may give their vows to each other in the strength of your steadfast love. Enable them to continue growing in love and peace with you and with one another all the days of their lives. Amen.

(Chip to Gretchen)

You glow with an inner and outer beauty. Your smile melts the toughest situation, and your embrace warms me up on the coldest night. When I look at you, I see a person confident in herself, who glows in any circumstance, whose fortitude and strength allows you to remain grounded in God when the storms come. I see a heart aching to help others, a heart that is able to conquer a situation that most would have withdrawn from. You overextend yourself due to kindness, and rely on God and me to carry you through. Your faith is childlike in belief and growing with hunger through each experience and day. You clearly have a light lit by the Lord. You live to have joy in each day. You challenge me to be a better husband, father, and man. You have touched the inner parts of my heart and soul that only God has been able to reach and dwell. This has caused me to be the man who stands before you, and I am very happy with whom I have become. You are my biggest supporter, and I confide all things in you. You are the other half of my heart, and complete me in every way. Being connected with you so deeply and emotionally ensures that you can both give me my greatest feelings of joy and deepest hurt. You make my heart skip a beat every time I come home and see you smile when you see me, even ten years later. You cause my heart to ache when I see you in pain and anguish. I want to hold you, fix it all, wrap my arms around you, and prevent anything and everyone from hurting you. All of these God-Blessed traits make me feel undeserving of you. I am blessed that God has allowed us to share our lives together.

(Gretchen to Chip)

You are my best friend, with whom I share my dreams, playtime, and prayer time. I share my everything with you. In you, I can see a breath-taking image of God's love for me. He was incredible in how he created only you for me, how you loved me endlessly when I could not even find myself. You tried to put my pieces back together to make me whole again. You've held my hand in the darkness and numbness to pull me back into the light of Christ. We have endured excessive trials together with great strength and victory – as God has intended. I love you with my entire soul and spirit, a place that only you and God may reside! Thank you for marrying me again. My vow to you is that I can give back to you all that you are and all that you have given me—and much, more, with the help of God. I love you.

(**Brenda**) Chip and Gretchen have rings as the outward symbols of their ongoing commitment to each other. From earliest times, the ring has been a symbol of wedded love. An unbroken and never-ending circle symbolizes a commitment to love that is also never ending. Chip and Gretchen have decided to do hand blessing and lasso ceremonies in place of the ring exchange, because they already exchanged rings ten years ago.

HAND BLESSING CEREMONY:

(**Pastor**) Gretchen, please hold Chip's hands palms up, so you may see the gift that they have been and are to you.

These are the hands of your best friend, young and strong and vibrant with love, that is holding yours on this day, as he promises to continue passionately loving and cherishing you through the years, for a lifetime of happiness.

These are the hands that have and will continue to work alongside yours, as together you continue to build your future, as you laugh and cry as you share your innermost secrets and dreams.

These are the hands that have, and will continue to, countless times wipe the tears from your eyes: tears of sorrow and tears of joy.

These are the hands that have and will continue to comfort you in illness, and hold you when fear or grief engulfs your heart.

These are the hands that when wrinkled and aged will still be reaching for yours, still giving you the same unspoken tenderness with just a touch.

These are the hands that will tenderly lift your chin and brush your cheek as they raise your face to look into his eyes: eyes that are filled completely with his overwhelming love and desire for you.

Chip, please hold Gretchen's hands palms up, so you may see the gift that they are to you.

These are the hands of your best friend, smooth, young and carefree, that are holding yours on this day, as she promises to continue passionately loving and cherishing you through the years, for a lifetime of happiness.

These are the hands that have and will continue to massage tension from you neck and back in the evenings after you've both had a long hard day.

These are the hands that have and will continue to hold you tight as you struggle through difficult times.

These are the hands that have and will continue to comfort you when you are sick, or console you when you are grieving.

These are the hands that when wrinkled and aged will still be reaching for yours, still giving you the same unspoken tenderness with just a touch.

These are the hands that will give you support as she encourages you to chase down your dreams.

Together as a team, everything you wish for can be realized and attained with the help of God.

LASSO CEREMONY:

(**Pastor**, place the lasso around Chip and Gretchen's wrists in a figure eight while explaining the following)

The lasso, placed around the wrists of Chip and Gretchen, and shaped in an infinity symbol, symbolizes their love and eternity of marriage. Both Chip and Gretchen must equally shoulder the responsibilities that a marriage brings. They pledge to support each other in love, joy and sorrow.

Chip repeat after me – From this day on, I recommit myself to you, your ring and this lasso are symbols of my pledge.

Gretchen repeat after me - From this day on, I recommit myself to you, your ring and this lasso are symbols of my pledge.

God, bless these hands that you see before you this day. May they always be held by one another. Give them the strength to hold on during the storms of stress and the dark of disillusionment. Keep them tender and gentle as they nurture each other in their wondrous love. Help these hands to continue building a relationship founded in your grace, rich in caring, and devoted in reaching for your perfection. May Chip and Gretchen see their four hands as healer, protector, shelter and guide. We ask this in Jesus name, Amen.

SAND BLENDING CEREMONEY:

(Brenda)

Chip and Gretchen, may your love always be as constant as the never-ending waves, flowing endlessly from the depths of the sea. Just as the waters touch and nourish the many shores of the earth, may your love be a moving sea between the shores of your souls. Just as there will never be a morning without the ocean's flow, there will never be a day without your love for each other.

The first shell represents you Chip, in all that you were, all that you are as part of a couple, and all that you will ever be, and the other shell represents you Gretchen, in all that you were, all that you are as part of a couple and all that you will ever be. The brown sand in the bottom of the bottle represents Christ, who is your life's foundation. Each one holds its own unique beauty, strength, and character. They can stand on their own with Christ and be whole, without need of anything else. However, after these three are blended together they will create an entirely new and extraordinarily more intricate entity. Each grain of sand brings to the mixture a lasting beauty that forever enriches the combination.

Please pour the sand into this common container to symbolize your oneness.

This container of sand represents the last ten years and your future lives together. Just as these grains of sand can never be separated and poured again into the individual containers, so is your marriage a molding of two individual personalities, bonded together forming one heart and one love in Christ.

Walk the leis to the ocean and toss them out to share this day with your deceased relatives and friends. Place the wreath in the ocean with all of your combined past trials, hardships, pain, and disappointments of the past. Allow Christ to take them, freeing yourselves, from this day forward, of old baggage. Out with the old. In with the new.

May the sun bring you new energy by day. May the moon softly restore you by night. May the rain wash away your worries. And may you live the days of your lives in peace, love, and happiness.

(Pastor) you may choose to add a prayer here if you'd like... your choice

Chip and Gretchen, having witnessed your vows of affirmation with God, all who are assembled here, and by the authority of love itself, I do affirm that you have expressed your desire to continue as husband and wife.

You may now kiss your bride.

Ladies and Gentleman, it is my honor to present to you, once again as husband and wife: Lieutenant Commander and Mrs. Chip Walker

Thank you for reading. I hope you enjoyed my story
and found hope from what you've read.
If you want to contact me, go to:
coachingbyphoebe.com
myseasidecreations.com
or e-mail me at
phoebe@myseasidecreations.com

My friend Wanda took family photos for us December 2014.
My family from left to right, Ryan, Gretchen,
Ashley, TJ, Chip

PHOEBE A Walker

www.ingramcontent.com/pod-product-compliance
Lightning Source LLC
Chambersburg PA
CBHW070343090426
42733CB00009B/1273